D0553909

NATURE'S MASTERPIECE

*The Brain
and How it Works*

Other books by J. Lawrence Pool:

The Early Diagnosis and Treatment of Acoustic Nerve Tumors
Aneurysms and Arteriovenous Malformations of the Brain
Izaak Walton. The Compleat Angler and His Turbulent Times
History of the Neurological Institute of New York
Your Brain and Nerves
America's Valley Forges and Valley Furnaces

NATURE'S MASTERPIECE

The Brain and How it Works

J. Lawrence Pool
M.D., D. Med. Sci.

Walker and Company
New York

First published in the United States of America
in 1986 by the Walker Publishing Company, Inc.

Published simultaneously in Canada by John Wiley & Sons
Canada, Limited, Rexdale, Ontario.

Library of Congress Cataloging-in-Publication Data

Pool, J. Lawrence (James Lawrence), 1906–
  Nature's masterpiece.

  Bibliography: p.
  Includes index.
  1. Brain.   I. Title.
QP376.P655   1986   612'.82   86–13248
ISBN 0-8027-0916-8
ISBN 0-8027-7298-6 (pbk.)

Printed in the United States of America

Book design by Nancy Field

10 9 8 7 6 5 4 3 2 1

To my wife Angeline

Contents

Acknowledgments

R. Campbell James of Washington, D.C., Sarah Burnham of Asheville, North Carolina, and Garrett Borque of Jefferson, Maine, kindly read the manuscript for the book. Their suggestions, from the layman's point of view, have been incorporated in the text.

For invaluable technical suggestions I am deeply indebted to Dr. Edgar M. Housepian, Professor of Neurological Surgery at the College of Physicians and Surgeons (P & S), Columbia University, and his son, Dr. David Housepian, a recent P & S graduate. Professor Edward B. Schlesinger kindly contributed data on current developments in scan tests.

Dr. James E. Finn, Chief of Neurosurgery at the Waterbury Hospital, Waterbury, Connecticut, and a former resident of mine, generously provided items for some of the illustrations in the book. Mrs. Francis H. O'Brien, electroencephalographer of the Waterbury Hospital, graciously supplied the EEG tracings.

I am particularly grateful to Neil O. Hardy, professional medical illustrator of Westport, Connecticut, for his superb anatomical renderings.

To my wife Angeline, I extend the warmest thanks for all the time and care she devoted to editorial work throughout the initial preparation of the text.

J. Lawrence Pool, M.D.

List of Illustrations

NATURE'S MASTERPIECE

*The Brain
and How it Works*

When Nature her great masterpiece designed,
And framed her last, best work, the human mind . . .

—ROBERT BURNS

CHAPTER 1

Your Private Computer

The magic of your mind—the magic that lets you enjoy family and friends, fun and games, and do all the things you "have a mind" to do—depends on your private computer: your brain. Your very life depends on it. It keeps your lungs breathing and controls your heartbeat, even when you are asleep, and its thermostat keeps your body from getting dangerously hot or cold.

While this private computer may not be able to guide spaceships to the stars or multiply a hundred numbers in a split second, it programs just about everything you do, whether it's thinking, talking, moving an arm or leg, or understanding what you see, hear, and feel.

The nerve cells of its gray matter are its "chips." Unlike the chips of a manmade computer, they make emotions possible—love, joy, fear, anger, and sorrow—and they generate their own electricity.

1

Our private computers begin life in the embryo as a thin layer of cells: nerve cells and others that support them. Wasting no time, these cells start growing at the rate of one hundred to one thousand cells a minute, according to neurobiologist W. Maxwell Cowan. During the last months before a baby is born, they grow at the astonishing rate of 250,000 cells (that's a quarter of a million) every minute.

As this first layer of cells grows larger and thicker, its edges gradually curl into a tube-shaped structure. The head of this "tube" gradually blossoms into the shape and form of the adult brain. The tail end forms the spinal cord, which connects the brain to the nerves of the body. By the time a baby is born, the brain has developed nearly all the nerve cells it will ever have—100 billion of them. The brain, however, keeps growing larger, until a child is about eight years old, because of the growth of the cells that support the brain, *and* the growth of more branches of the nerve fibers that are the "wires" of the brain.

What about the development of the skull, the box in which the brain is so neatly wrapped and packaged? The skull is not, as some people think, one piece of bone, but is made up of several pieces, all different shapes and sizes. They include the forehead bone, the large bone at the back of the head, the bones on each side of the head, and those at the base of the skull.

In a baby these sections of the skull are thin, soft, flat islands of cartilage that are not yet bone or even joined together. As a child grows, they expand until their edges touch and then fit neatly together like pieces of a jigsaw puzzle. During this process each piece of cartilage slowly gets harder and thicker until it is solid bone. In addition, tiny toothlike cogs sprout from the edges of each piece. By the time a child is three years old, these tiny cogs have fitted snugly in between those on the bones next to them, thus locking all the skull bones tightly together (Figure 1). These connections make the brain box extra strong so that, like a helmet, it protects the brain from bumps and bruises that might otherwise injure it.

The skull itself is well packaged—first by a thin layer of something that looks like moist tissue paper (doctors, in fact, call it tissue) and, over this covering, some muscles, then your scalp and the skin of your forehead.

Some of the muscles covering the skull are in your forehead, like those you use to frown or raise your eyebrows. Others, behind your ears, are like those a rabbit uses to make its ears stand up. (Some people can wiggle their ears with those muscles.) Then there are muscles at the

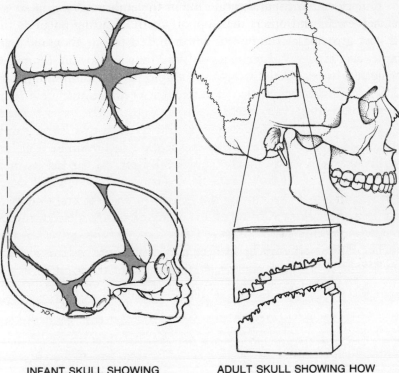

INFANT SKULL SHOWING
ISLANDS OF CARTILAGE

ADULT SKULL SHOWING HOW
BONES LOCK TOGETHER

Figure 1. Formation and locking of skull bones.

back of the head to hold it up and move it back and forth or to one side.

Inside the skull there are three wrappings around the brain. They are called the *meninges* (men-IN-jees), Latin for "membranes." Infection of the meninges results in meningitis, a serious illness that can lead to high fever, stiffness of the neck, and inability to think and behave normally. It is usually fatal unless promptly treated by antibiotics.

The outermost membrane is also the lining of the skull. It is light blue and is as stiff as a sheet of parchment. It is so tough and durable that it is called the *dura*. Its two layers, arranged like the criss-cross layers of plywood, account for its toughness. A surgeon can peel a piece of the outer layer from the inner layer to patch a hole elsewhere in the dura caused by a serious fracture.

Under the dura are two thin transparent membranes that are held in place by tiny strands resembling those of a spider's web. Because of their spidery attachments they are called the *arachnoid* (meaning "spiderlike") membranes.

The innermost arachnoid membrane is so thin and moist that it clings to the curves and contours of the brain like a wet see-through bathing suit. It is kept moist by a small amount of brain fluid, as clean and clear as spring water, that circulates between the arachnoid membranes surrounding it (Figure 2).

The brain fluid comes from pink tufts of tissue inside four narrow caves, called *ventricles,* deep down in the core of the brain. The fluid flows from one cave to another and finally out of the last cave, the fourth ventricle, at the back of the head. From there it flows all around the brain and also down around the *spinal cord.* It is therefore known as *cerebrospinal fluid,* or CSF for short. Some of this fluid seeps through the entire substance of the brain.

The fluid is drained, by little tufts of tissue, into veins around the brain (Figure 3). If it is not properly drained, or if too much is produced, a condition known as "water on the brain" (properly called

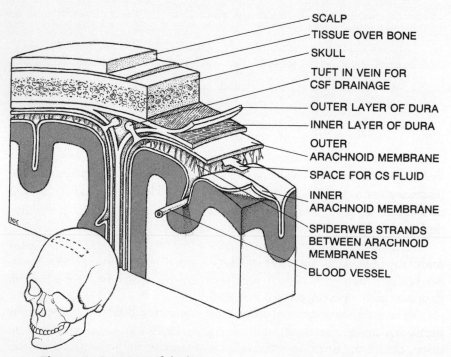

Figure 2. Coverings of the brain.

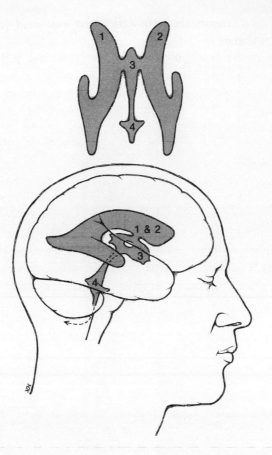

Figure 3. Fluid-filled cavities: The ventricles of the brain.

hydrocephalus) results. One operation for curing this condition is the placement of a permanent valve in the head. The valve, about the size of a dime, keeps the fluid pressure at a safe, normal level. A slender flexible tube attached to the valve drains fluid into a vein.

CSF keeps the brain moist and clean by bathing it and helps maintain the proper amount of natural salts and chemicals the brain needs. By acting as a sort of water jacket, this fluid also cushions the brain, to some extent, from jolting injuries.

Yet another source of protection from such jolts are the two partitions inside the skull, which are made of the same tough blue tissue, the dura, that lines the skull. They protect the brain in much the same way that partitions in an egg box cushion eggs from damage.

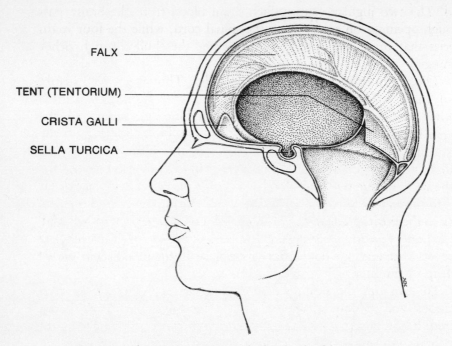

FALX

TENT (TENTORIUM)

CRISTA GALLI

SELLA TURCICA

Figure 4. The two partitions in the head: The falx and tent.

One partition runs all the way from the front to the back of the head in the middle of the skull. This wall between the two halves of the brain has a curved sickle shape and is therefore called the *falx*, Latin for "sickle." Its forward end is anchored to a thin piece of bone behind the nose that is called the *crista galli*, meaning "rooster's crest" (Figure 4).

The second partition stretches across the back half of the skull from one side to the other in the shape of a *tent*. The largest and uppermost part of the brain, the *cerebrum*, sits on top of the tent. Two smaller parts of the brain are under the tent. They are the *cerebellum* or "little brain," and the *brain stem*, described in the next chapter.

Along the bottom of the skull there are a number of openings. Some are about as big around as a lead pencil; others are smaller and a few are larger. The nerves of the head, the *cranial nerves* (which I'll describe later), pass through some of these openings on their way to and from the eyes, face, mouth, ears, and other parts of the head.

The spinal cord passes through the largest opening, about the size of a fifty-cent piece, which is in the base of the skull at the back of the head. The two jugular veins, which drain blood from the brain, pass through openings on each side of the spinal cord, while the four main arteries that carry blood to the brain enter the skull through other openings.

The brain, incidentally, is a fuel guzzler. Though it weighs only about three pounds (a mere 2 percent or less of an average adult's weight), the brain requires a great deal of blood to supply all the oxygen and sugar it burns. Twenty percent of all blood pumped by the heart (one out of every five quarts) goes to the brain, according to Leslie L. Iverson, neurochemist. The oxygen in this blood is essential for all the brain's functions, and blood sugar is its main source of energy. It can, for instance, burn up as much sugar during prolonged mental work as the muscles do during prolonged exercise. That is why we may get as hungry working long hours at a desk as we do from playing three sets of tennis; our bodies have to replace all the blood sugar we've used up in thinking.

To sum up, the skull, its outer and inner wrappings, its two partitions, and its water jacket all help protect the brain from being injured. If you bump your head, the outside of it may hurt a little, but your brain will usually be unharmed.

Now let's see what the brain looks like.

The brain is a world consisting of a number of unexplored continents and great stretches of unknown territory.

—RAMON Y CAJAL,
Spanish neuroanatomist, 1852–1934.

CHAPTER 2

What Does the Brain Look Like?

When I asked two young boys to describe the brain, one replied, "It's something you think with." But the other said, "It's just a bunch of muscles stuffed in the head." He was wrong. There are no muscles *inside* the skull, and the brain does not look or feel like a muscle in any way.

Strange as it may seem, the upper part of the brain looks and feels like a mound of firm, opaque jelly that has just been turned out of a gelatin mold. The gray matter that covers the brain gives it its characteristic light gray color, and the fluid all around it makes it look clean, moist, and shiny.

If you looked down at the top of a person's brain (the *cerebrum*), you would see that it has two halves (called *hemispheres*) which are almost exactly alike, one on the right and one on the left, like the two

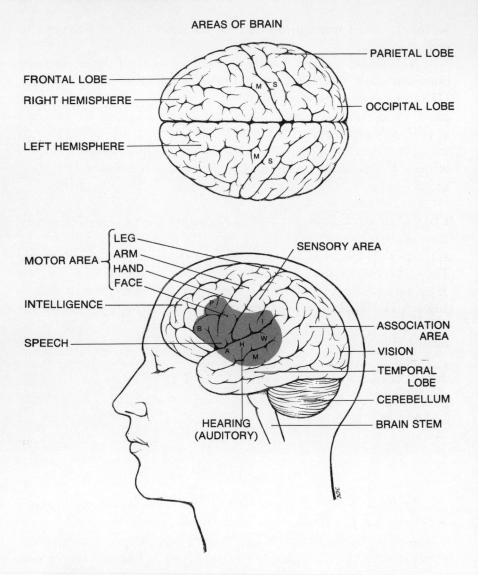

Figure 5. Lobes and surface areas of the brain.
A. Association area for words.
B. Broca's area for speaking or writing words.
H. Hearing (auditory) area for words.
I. Interpretation of words seen or heard.
M. Short-term memory for words.
P. Processing of words to be spoken or written.
W. Wernicke's area for initial interpretation of words seen or heard.

halves of a small watermelon that has been sliced in two from end to end.

You would also see that the surface, or *cortex,* of the cerebrum is bumpy-looking, covered with "humps" of different shapes and sizes. (Doctors call these humps *convolutions* or *gyri.*) Some humps are as long and thick as your little finger; others are short, curly, or triangular and as thick as your thumb. Their different shapes and sizes serve as landmarks that indicate where the speech, vision, and other important areas of the brain are located. Each hump consists of a thin rim of gray tissue and a good deal of white matter underneath.

These humps are not neatly lined up, side by side, like matches in a box of matches. They look more like the crumpled pleats of a gray sheet that has been stuffed into a shoebox. This is not surprising, for the gyri really are the pleats of a sheet—a sheet of closely packed nerve cells. The visible outer surface of each gyrus is from one half to three quarters of an inch wide. The two hidden sides of each gyrus, which extend down from the surface, are about the same size. This means that there is at least twice as much gray matter in the cortex as you can see on its surface (Figure 6).

If it were possible to unfold the gray matter that surrounds the three sides of all the humps of the brain and smooth it out, like ironing a crumpled sheet, it would be nearly large enough to cover a card table.

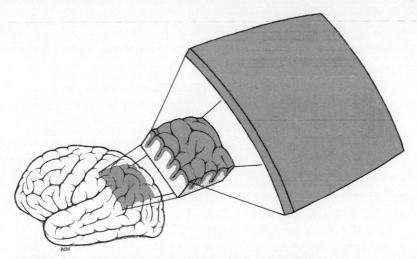

Figure 6. Pleats (gyri) of cortex unfolded (schematic).

Thus its "packaging" is quite economical, fitting a large amount of tissue into a very small space.

This "tablecloth"—the cortex of the brain—contains 70 percent, or nearly three quarters, of all the nerve cells of the entire brain, as pointed out by neuroanatomist Walle J. H. Nauta. They are the cells that make it possible for us to think, see, hear, smell, taste, talk, and move our muscles. Some of them interpret sensations such as feelings of heat, cold, and pain. Others make it possible for us to control our emotions, to learn and remember.

The cortex is the newest part of the brain, in terms of evolution, and is the command post for the deeper, older parts of the brain underneath, which are described in the next chapter. Because of its color and its role in thinking, the cortex is commonly called the *gray matter.* The cortex, however, is not the only part of the brain that is gray. All parts of the brain—and for that matter, of the spinal cord—are gray wherever nerve cells are packed closely together.

The cortex of each half of the cerebrum forms four *lobes:* the right and left frontal lobes, the temporal lobes under each temple, the parietal (or wall-like) lobes behind the frontal lobes, and the occipital (or hindmost) lobes at the back of the head.

In each hemisphere of the brain, midway between the front and back of the brain (as shown in Figure 5), a strip of cortex, the *motor area* (M), controls the muscles of the *opposite* side of the body. Immediately behind it another strip, the *sensory area* (S), registers sensations from the opposite side of the body. This is because the nerve fibers of each motor and sensory area cross over from one side to the other on their way to and from the spinal cord (Figure 9).

Each motor and sensory area, finally, has small sections in it for the face, fingers, hands, legs, and feet that form a map of opposite parts of the body, as shown in Figure 5.

Brain surgeons make good use of this knowledge during operations close to a motor area. Although they know the location of each motor area, they must check its limits to be absolutely sure they are right, for injury to a motor area could cause weakness or even paralysis of the opposite hand, arm, or leg.

To find these limits, the surgeon touches the surface of the brain with the tips of two fine wires that carry a weak electrical current—barely enough to light a pocket flashlight. When the wires touch a motor area (Figure 7), the current stimulates nerve cells in a way that

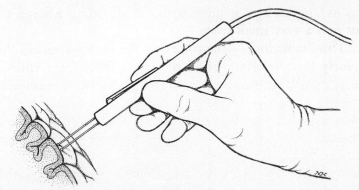

Figure 7. Stimulation of cortex to localize function (cut-away view).

makes the opposite cheek, hand, arm, or leg move a little. This harmless but important test shows the surgeon *exactly* where the motor area is located. He then lays a moist cotton pad over it to protect it from any possible harm while he operates.

The speech area, which we use to plan, speak, write, and understand words, surrounds the lower portion of one of the motor areas. In right-handed people it is on the left side of the brain and in left-handed people on the right side.

The senses of smell, taste, and hearing are registered in each temporal lobe, under each temple of the head (Figure 5).
the brain. Other parts of the cortex, known as *association areas*, organize and exchange information, coordinate activities of the brain, and play a role in planning and thinking. Their functions are not as well understood as those of the other areas. They might be thought of as the "great stretches of unknown territory" mentioned in the quotation at the opening of this chapter.

The *white matter* of the brain, which is under the cortex, is made up partly of the special cells that support and hold the brain together, and partly of the nerve fibers that connect nerve cells and form the wiring system of the brain.

The exact origin and destinations of most of these nerve fibers have been discovered and mapped in blueprint form as the result of more than one hundred years of slow, careful research relying on the use of the microscope and special dyes. Modern methods for charting the course of these nerve fibers include the injection of fluorescent dyes that make the nerve fibers literally shine in the dark.

Within the book and volume of thy brain . . .
—HAMLET I, V, 103

CHAPTER 3

The Depths
of the Brain

The brain could not possibly carry out all its many functions without the help of parts of it that are underneath the cerebral cortex and other parts that are under the partition at the back of the head called the tent (Fig. 3).

In the core of the brain, somewhat like seeds in the core of an apple, there are islands of gray matter made up of nerve cells. These islands or clusters of nerve cells vary in size and shape from that of an almond to that of a plum and each has a twin in the opposite side of the brain. They are called *basal ganglia* (Figures 8 and 9) because they are close to the base of the brain.

Long before their functions were even guessed they were given simple, homely names by doctors many years ago whose common language was Latin. Here are their Latin and English names: *caudate,* tail-like; *putamen,* shell-like; *globus pallidus,* pale globe; and *amygdala,* almond.

The basal ganglia, each in its own way, play an important role in initiating and controlling muscle movements and in modulating and relaying sensations. Some of them also share in the control of emotional reactions.

Certain diseases of the basal ganglia upset circuits that control muscle movements to such an extent that distressing contortions of the

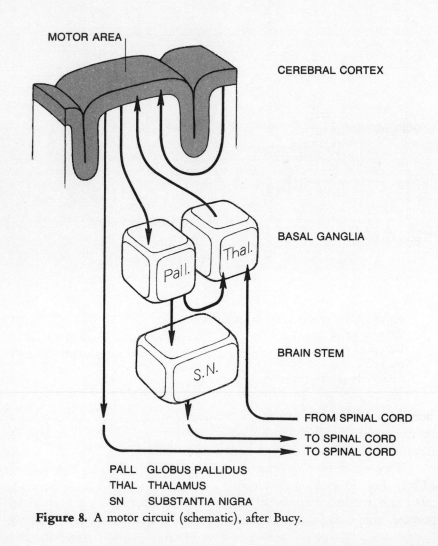

PALL   GLOBUS PALLIDUS
THAL   THALAMUS
SN   SUBSTANTIA NIGRA

Figure 8. A motor circuit (schematic), after Bucy.

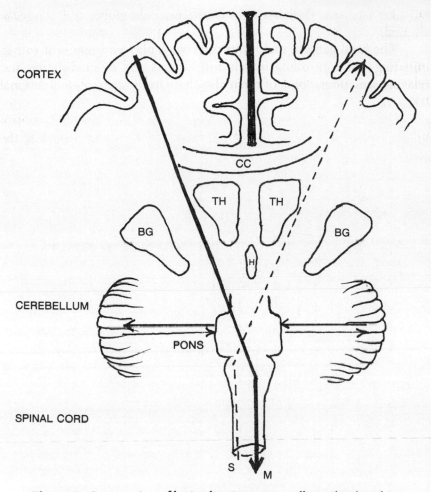

CORTEX

CC

TH   TH

BG   BG

H

CEREBELLUM

PONS

SPINAL CORD

S   M

Figure 9. Cross-section of brain showing corpus callosum(CC) and the crossing of motor(M) and sensory(S) pathways. Th: Thalamus. BG: Basal ganglia. H: Hypothalamus. Pons: Part of the brain stem (for cerebellar connections). M: Descending motor pathway (solid line). S: Ascending sensory pathway (dotted line).

face, arms, and legs occur. Some ailments of these kinds can be relieved by stereotaxic needling of the brain (see Chapter 13) to interrupt the transmission of abnormal nerve signals to the muscles.

Two other deep clusters of nerve cells, the right and left *thalamus* (Th in Fig. 9) share in the control of muscle movements. They also relay and modulate information concerning sensations such as bodily posture, vision, and pain. Constant severe pain can be relieved by deliberately destroying or electrically stimulating the very small, specific subdivision of a thalamus that is concerned with pain. This, too, is done by stereotaxic needling, described in Chapter 13, which does not have any significant effects on any other function of the brain.

Two other structures deep in the brain, one on the right and the other on the left, are each the size and shape of a little seahorse. For this reason they were given the name of *hippocampus,* from the Greek words *hippo* (horse) and *campus* (sea creature). Their importance will be discussed in the chapter on memory.

The two parts of the brain under the partition at the back of the head, the tent (see Figure 4), are the cerebellum or "little brain," and beneath that, the brain stem (Figure 10).

The right and left halves of the cerebellum are each about the size of a tennis ball. They are connected to each other, to the cortex of the cerebrum above them, and to the brain stem below them by thick bundles of nerve fibers. The surface gyri of the cerebellum are narrower, more uniform in size, and more neatly arranged than those of the cortex of the upper part of the brain.

The cerebellum mainly controls balance and the smooth action of muscles. It enables us to walk and run without stumbling or staggering and to do all sorts of things that require skill, speed, and perfect timing, whether we're playing the piano or playing basketball. The cerebellum also helps parts of the brain above it do their own work in a smooth, efficient manner.

The brain stem has a shape and size somewhat like that of the stem of a large plant or vegetable. The forward end of the brain stem, technically known as the *midbrain,* is connected to the lower part of the brain. Its hindmost end, the *medulla,* is connected to the spinal cord. In the middle of the brain stem there is a bulge known as the *pons,* (Latin for "bridge"), which consists of large bundles of nerve fibers that connect the two halves of the cerebellum (Figures 9 and 10).

The brain stem is extremely important for two reasons. First, *all* the nerve signals, the messages between the brain and the body, pass through it. Second, it contains many small but very important groups of nerve cells that *keep us alive.* For instance, one group of these nerve cells enables the lungs to take in air, and another enables them to exhale. A third group regulates the heartbeat, and a fourth the blood pressure. If these life-preserving cells are destroyed, the result is instant death. That is why in a bullfight, a toreador aims his sword at the spot where the bull's brain stem is located.

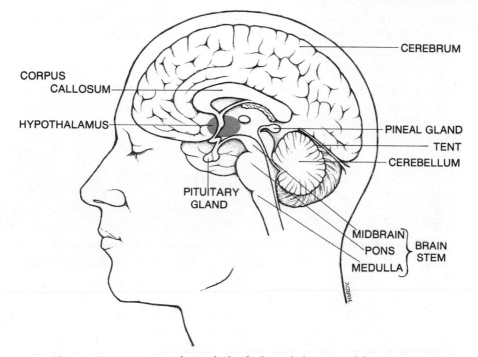

Figure 10. Pituitary and pineal glands, hypothalamus, and brain stem.

If the brain stem is seriously but not totally damaged, the nerve cells in it that keep us awake and alert may cease to function, resulting in the unconscious vegetable-like state known as a *coma.*

Other small groups of nerve cells in the brain stem are connected to the nerves that control the eyes, facial muscles, mouth, and throat. Sensations, such as touch and pain felt by the face, taste, and sounds, are received and relayed to the brain by still other cell stations in the brain stem. Olive-shaped groups, appropriately called the *olives,* are connected to the cerebellum to help control our balance and muscle coordination. All these groups of nerve cells are gray because, as stated earlier, wherever nerve cells are packed closely together, they make that part of the brain look gray.

On each side of the brain stem, however, there is a blue, a red, and a black group of nerve cells. The blue group, the *locus caeruleus,* or blue spot, releases chemical substances that play an important role in keeping the brain active and alert. The *red nucleus,* and the *substantia nigra* (or black substance) are parts of motor circuits that keep our muscles moving smoothly and easily. The substantia nigra releases a chemical called dopamine, which is especially important in this regard. When it fails to function, muscles become stiff and shaky, as in the distressing ailment known as Parkinson's disease.

Circuits that control muscle movements, as indicated in Figure 8, include the motor cortex, some of the basal ganglia, and the substantia nigra in the brain stem. Other, different motor circuits include connections with the cerebellum, as shown by Professor Paul. C. Bucy, neurosurgeon, in 1944.

Between the brain stem and the basal ganglia, there is a small, extremely important portion of the brain concerned with life-sustaining functions. It controls the brain-stem cells that regulate the heartbeat, blood pressure, and intestinal activities and is the headquarters for the *autonomic system* of nerves (described in Chapter 8). It is also concerned with hunger, thirst, kidney output, the amount of sugar and fat in the blood, emotions and emotional reactions, body temperature, and control of certain glands.

This vital portion of the brain sends and receives nerve signals to and from parts of the brain above, below, and to each side of it. It is therefore a sort of Times Square for the "uptown," "downtown," and "crosstown" transmission of its signals.

It is located over the pituitary gland (which is discussed in the next chapter) and under the thalamus, one of the basal ganglia. It is therefore known as the *hypothalamus,* meaning under the thalamus (Figures 9 and 10). Adjacent to it (but not shown in the figures) is a small area, known as the *septum,* which shares in many of the functions of the hypothalamus.

To illustrate how just one of the many small but powerful nerve-cell stations in the hypothalamus works, let us consider the station that regulates body temperature, the "thermostat" of the brain.

The thermostat controls body temperature by making us sweat to cool off and shiver to warm up. By shutting down the flow of blood through the skin (thus making the skin pale) it conserves body heat. By allowing a lot of blood to flow through the skin (thus making the skin flushed), the blood is cooled by the outside air, thus reducing body heat.

The next chapter considers the glands of the brain—the pituitary, or master gland, and the pineal gland, or "third eye."

What is our life? A play of passion . . .

—SIR WALTER RALEIGH

CHAPTER 4

The Master Gland
and the Third Eye

The master gland of the brain, the *pituitary*, and the *pineal gland*, or "third eye," are endocrine glands which pour chemicals called hormones into the bloodstream.

The pituitary gland is under the brain, a short distance behind the eyes, where it sits in a cup of bone about the size of a lima bean called the *Turk's saddle*. The gland is connected to the brain by a slender stalk (see Figure 10). Nerve fibers in this stalk control the output of some (but not all) of the gland's hormones. Small blood vessels in the stalk convey pituitary hormones to large blood vessels nearby. The circulating blood then carries the hormones to parts of the brain and body where they are needed.

The gland has three distinct parts, each of which is composed of different kinds of cells for the output of different hormones.

21

Small as it is, the pituitary makes a surprisingly large number of powerful hormones. One of them helps regulate our blood pressure, another adjusts our sense of thirst, and still another makes our bodies grow (were it not for this growth hormone, we would be dwarfs).

A fourth hormone stimulates the thyroid gland, which keeps the body's metabolism active, and a fifth stimulates the cortex of the adrenal glands, which makes natural cortisone, a hormone that helps keep body tissues healthy. Other pituitary hormones control the sex glands and the various stages of pregnancy (Kalman D. Post, neurosurgeon, et al). Still other chemical substances manufactured by the pituitary influence the transmission of nerve signals in the brain, especially those concerned with emotional reactions and sensations of pain.

The pineal gland is about the size of a large pea and is tucked between the two halves of the brain at about the middle of the head (Figure 10). Although it cannot see, it is called the third eye because it responds to light. Slender nerves from the eyes keep it informed of light and darkness.

The existence of this gland has been known for nearly two thousand years, but only in the past twenty years or so has its function been clearly understood. When the great Greco-Roman physician Galen described it sometime around 150 A.D., he referred to it as the "gatekeeper" of the brain fluid, controlling its flow as a sluice gate controls a stream of water. In 1640 the French philosopher Descartes thought it was the seat of the soul because it was the only isolated structure in the head not connected to the brain and therefore had to be a very special organ.

Early in this century the pineal was generally thought to be a useless vestigial part of the body, like the appendix, because in humans it so often becomes calcified with age. This notion was abandoned when it was found that children with tumors of the pineal gland become sexually precocious and that in lower animals it is sensitive to changes in light. Research has now shown that when amphibians, fish, fowls, and other animals are in the dark, as during long dark winter days or at night, the pineal gland secretes a powerful hormone, *melatonin*, that inhibits sexual activity. This gland thus influences the seasonal as well as the daily sexual activity of animals, according to Waldhauser and Wurtman, neurophysiologists. Bright light, on the other hand, causes the gland to stop making this hormone. The sex glands then become active. This is why farmers use artificial light in chicken coops at night. The brightness increases the hens' laying of eggs.

Proof of the effect of light on the pineal has been shown by experiments in which the nerves connecting the eyes to this gland were cut. The pineal then no longer responds to darkness and stops pouring out its slow-down hormone. Sex glands then become so active that, for instance, sheep breed more often than they usually do and fish breed out of their regular breeding season as well as during it.

Does the same effect occur in humans? And if so, what happens to people like Eskimos who live in excessive darkness in winter and excessive light in summer? Dr. Joel E. Ehrenkranz, who spent a number of years studying the Intuit Indians in Labrador found that yearly birth rates occurred in a regular pattern, peaking in March. He matched this pattern with the hormonal activity of the pineal gland by taking blood samples from Intuit hunters at regular intervals and testing the samples for melatonin.

Dr. Ehrenkranz found that the production of melatonin varied throughout the year, achieving its highest levels during the darkness of winter and its lowest during the bright days of summer. A check against birth records showed that conception was least frequent when the hormone was at its highest levels. In other words, there was less sexual activity during dark days because darkness made the pineal gland pour out more melatonin than usual, which reduced sexual interest. So this research indicates that the third eye does govern the sex glands of humans as well as of other animals; and other scientists have done work that gives further proof of this phenomenon.

With respect to the quotation heading this chapter, it is clear that the pineal and pituitary glands, by profoundly influencing the activity of the sex glands, can affect the "play of passion" in both animals and humans.

The cells composing the pineal and pituitary glands differ from each other and from the two families of cells that form the brain. Those two "families" are the subject of the next chapter.

A cell state, *in which every cell is a citizen* . . .

—RUDOLF VIRCHOW,
German pathologist, 1821–1902

CHAPTER 5

The Two Families
of Brain Cells

Just as the Milky Way is made up of millions upon millions of stars, so the three-pound human brain is made up of millions upon millions of cells. In total, there are some 100 billion nerve cells and 200 billion supporting cells, plus trillions of nerve fibers to connect the nerve cells, according to Nauta and Feirtag.

Brain cells, like all other cells of the body, are so small that they can be seen only with a microscope. Thousands would easily fit on the head of a pin. And, like "the citizens of a state," they have different shapes and sizes and different kinds of work to do.

Basically, though, there are two families of brain cells: *glial cells* and *neurons.* Glial cells, from *glia,* Latin for "glue," support the brain and hold it together, much the way beams and girders hold up a skyscraper. They do their work by means of slender strands, far finer than those of a spider's web, which reach out in all directions to join the strands of other glial cells. All these interwoven strands form the meshlike scaffolding that holds the brain together and is part of its white matter. (The rest of the white matter is composed of nerve fibers, which transmit the brain's nerve signals).

Many glial cells, far from being simply the beams and girders of the brain, are extraordinarily active. Some play a role in adjusting the chemistry of the brain. Others rove around its framework, keeping it clean. These are scavenger cells which, like tiny vacuum cleaners, suck up or engulf bits of old or injured tissue and dump them into the nearest vein to be carried away by the bloodstream. And there are some very small glial cells that coat nerve fibers with a white insulating substance called *myelin*. Glial cells also knit together injured parts of the brain by growing into a scar, and once in a great while, in a few people, they may grow so wildly, like a thick clump of weeds in the garden, that they form a tumor, a lump that must be removed by brain surgery.

Many glial cells even feed neurons. They do this by extracting sugar and other nourishing substances from brain arteries and transferring this fuel, in just the right amounts, to nearby neurons. These neurons might be compared to parents who hold a baby and feed it at the same time.

Ninety percent of the glial cells, resembling tiny stars, are *astrocytes*, meaning "star-shaped cells" (see Figure 11). Small and large cells of other shapes make up the remaining 10 percent.

Neurons, the brain's nerve cells, do the actual work of the brain. They are the cells that brought man out of the cave and made it possible for him to swing a golf club on the moon. Their job may seem more important than that of the glial cells, but without cooperation between the two families, the brain would not function at all.

Due to differences in size, shape, and function, there are more than two hundred varieties of neurons. Ninety-nine percent are relatively small, and most of them are located in the cortex where they are usually arranged in layers six cells deep. A few neurons of somewhat larger size occupy the middle layers of the gray matter of the cortex. (Figure 11). The largest neurons of the brain, some of which are shaped like baskets, are in the cerebellum, where they help us keep our balance.

Different arrangements of neurons fill the gray matter of the "humps" (the gyri) of the cortex. This means that the cortex is not

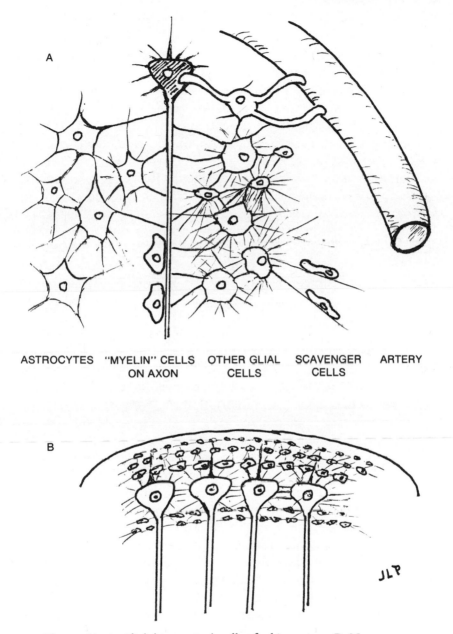

ASTROCYTES   "MYELIN" CELLS   OTHER GLIAL   SCAVENGER   ARTERY
            ON AXON   CELLS   CELLS

JLP

Figure 11. A: Glial (supporting) cells of white matter. B: Neurons (nerve cells) in gray matter of cerebral cortex.

uniformly wired, like the chips of a given make of computer. The visual area, for example, is different from the motor area, just as the motor area is different from the sensory and the speech areas, and so on. In addition, the basal ganglia, the cerebellum, and the brain stem are each wired differently and contain nerve cells that are different in size, shape, and function from those of the cortex.

Small as it is, a neuron is an extremely complicated unit. It not only generates its own electricity but also manufactures the chemicals it needs to speed its nerve signals on their way. Various odd-shaped particles inside the neurons are responsible for the cell's life and activities. Some particles are so small that they can be detected only by an electron miscroscope, which magnifies objects thousands of times their natural size. Certain very minute particles even travel up and down inside the nerve fibers of neurons to transport chemical substances the cell needs. Every neuron also contains a round or oval structure, its nucleus, which supervises its smaller parts. The master chemical in the nucleus is DNA (*de*-oxyribo-*n*ucleic *a*cid). Its inherited, coded genes automatically control the chemistry, metabolism, functions, and very life of the cell. Every neuron, in sum, is a tiny electrical power plant, a miniature chemical factory, and a busy message center, with a superintendent (its nucleus) in charge (Figure 12).

All around the outside of every neuron there are rather thick nerve fibers which divide into many thin whiskery branches (Figure 12). The ends of all these branches, and thousands of little sprouts along them, are in contact with neighboring nerve cells and their branches. A single neuron, therefore, depending on how many branching nerve fibers it has, may have anywhere from 1000 to 10,000 contacts called synapses, with other nerve cells and their nerve fibers.

These branching nerve fibers are the antennae of a nerve cell. Most of them receive nerve signals, although some send signals. They are known as *dendrites,* from the Latin word *dendron,* for tree, because of their many branches like the twigs of a tree (Figure 12) with thousands of sprouts or "spines" which make contact with other dendrites and also with axons and nerve cells.

A neuron sends its most important messages, like those which make an arm or leg move, by a single fiber. It is longer than a dendrite, is insulated by a thick coating of myelin, and is called an *axon,* from the Latin word for "axle" or "axis."

Axons vary in length. Axons that control the toes, for example, are so long that they extend all the way from a motor area at the top of the brain down to the lowermost portion of the spinal cord. Other

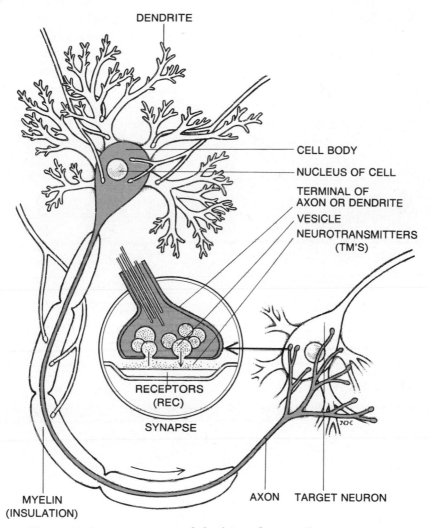

Figure 12. Synapses, axons, and dendrites of nerve cells.

axons, however, are so short that they extend merely from one gyrus to the next. Some axons, bunched together in large orderly bundles, link the front of the brain with its rear portions and the surface gray matter with the deep gray matter, the cerebellum, and the spinal cord. The right and left halves of the brain, finally, are connected by the largest bundle of all—the *corpus callosum* (See Figures 9 and 23), which extends from one side to the other under the entire length of the sickle-shaped partition called the falx. (Figure 4).

This is a highly simplified account of the two families of brain cells. It shows, however, what a marvellously complicated organ the brain is. A man-made computer is simple by comparison. Take a look at an advanced computer chip, which has only two connections, and compare it to a single nerve cell—which has anywhere from one thousand to ten thousand connections for exchanging its signals! As Carl Sagan put it, "A modern computer would have to be about ten thousand times larger in size than the human brain to handle the work that our brains do, even though a computer's signals are much faster."

And the whole earth is of one language.

—GENESIS 11:1

CHAPTER 6

Nerve Signals:
The Language of the Brain

The life and activities of all creatures of the earth, sea, and sky depend on nerve signals. They are the signals that make it possible for a snail to crawl, a fish to swim, a bird to fly, a dog to bark, and a man to walk, talk, and think. Perhaps the most remarkable thing about these signals is that they are all alike. A snail uses the *same kind* of nerve signals to crawl as you use to walk and talk. As neurobiologist Eric R. Kandel puts it, "There appear to be no fundamental differences in structure, chemistry or function between the neurons and synapses in man and those of a squid, a snail or a leech."

But what exactly *are* nerve signals? They are high-speed spiky electrical waves sent by nerve cells along the nerve fibers of the nerve cells to target cells of the brain, spinal cord, glands, and muscles and also to other dendrites and axons (Figure 12). The speeds at which the electrical waves travel depend on the size of nerve fibers and on how well they are insulated. Large, thick, well-insulated axons can handle as many as 600 signals per second at speeds of over 150 miles an hour— that's 220 feet per second. Thin, whiskery dendrites and small, poorly insulated axons conduct fewer signals per second at much slower speeds.

Nerve cells fire their signals in volleys, like bursts from a machine gun. The number of volleys and the rate of firing determine what happens when they reach their targets.

Chemical changes keep pace with each electrical wave as it races down a nerve fiber. They consist of extremely rapid exchanges of sodium and potassium ions between the inside and the outside of the nerve fiber. A nerve signal is therefore both an electrical and a chemical event.

Chemical changes of a different kind are necessary to transmit a nerve signal to a target cell, to another nerve fiber, or to a muscle or gland. This is because most dendrites and axons do not make direct contact with their targets. They end at a slitlike gap that separates them from a target cell or another nerve fiber. The gap is called a *synapse,* from the Greek word *synapsis,* meaning "junction."

The number of synapses in the brain is astronomical. For example, a cubic millimeter of the adult cortex, about the size of the head of a pin, contains approximately 10 trillion synapses.

The electrical wave of a nerve signal cannot jump across this gap the way a spark jumps the gap of a spark plug. How, then, is a nerve signal transmitted across a synapse? It is "ferried" across by special chemicals called *Trans*mitter substances (Kandel et al), or TMs for short.

TMs are stored in extremely small bubbles, called vesicles, at the ends of dendrites and axons. When the electrical wave of a nerve signal arrives at a vesicle, a flow of calcium ions makes the bubble burst, so to speak, like a punctured balloon. The transmitter substances are then discharged into the synapse.

The TMs scurry across the synapse to lodge in chemical "docks," on the surface of the target cell. These docks, which are protein mol-ecules, as neurochemist Solomon Snyder points out, are known as *receptors* (Rec in Figure 12). This sudden invasion of TMs makes the target cell generate fresh electrical waves to send the signal on its way.

There is a catch to this mechanism of transmission, however. Since there are at least thirty different kinds of TMs and receptors, TMs must fit into the receptors *perfectly,* like a key in a lock. Otherwise the signals will not go through. The brain relies on this principle to see that some signals are promptly transmitted while others are blocked.

Of the many different kinds of TMs, some are "general purpose" transmitters that either speed or block the transmission of nerve signals in many parts of the brain at the same time. Adrenaline-like substances, for example, speed signals on their way while another substance, called gamma amino butyric acid, (GABA for short) inhibits or blocks their transmission. There are even some TMs that speed signals in one circuit but block them in another.

Most TMs, however, are of the "special purpose" variety, meaning that they are made and used by specific circuits of the brain's wiring system for the transmission of *only* their own signals. The TMs of the circuit that keeps us awake and alert, for example, do not function in some of the circuits that keep our muscles moving smoothly, and vice versa.

While the transmission of nerve signals is controlled to a large extent by transmitter substances, STOP and GO cells—mostly small neurons—also control their transmission.

STOP, or *inhibitory*, nerve cells see to it that other neurons under their control do not go "haywire" and send such a flood of signals that, for instance, mental confusion or convulsions occur. The action of strychnine illustrates what happens when STOP cells do not function.

Strychnine is a deadly poison obtained from seeds of the East Indian tree *nux vomica* (nut-that-makes-one-vomit). Strychnine poisoning causes convulsions. So does the application of a drop of strychnine on an animal's brain. Doctors therefore thought it stimulated the brain, and for this reason they incorporated very small amounts of it in medicines, used for many years as tonics, which we might call pep pills, and even as heart stimulants.

Professor Dominick Purpura, now Dean of the Albert Einstein College of Medicine, New York, showed that strychnine is not a stimulant at all. He proved that it poisoned the small inhibitory cells immediately above the motor (or muscle-moving) cells of the brain's cortex. The motor cells, suddenly unleashed from the restraining influence of STOP cells, went wild. They sent out so many signals that convulsions occurred. Strychnine, in other words, was not a stimulant. It simply poisoned inhibitory cells.

GO, or activating, cells see to it that neurons under their control do not "sleep at the switch" but send out their signals promptly and vigorously when they are supposed to do so. The cells of the activating or alerting system of the brain are prime examples. It is the system or circuit that extends from the brain stem up to other parts of the brain, as stated in Chapter 3, to keep us awake and alert.

So the constant fine-tuning of brain circuits depends on several factors: teamwork between activating, or GO, and inhibitory, or STOP, cells; an interplay of activating and blocking transmitter substances (TMs); and finally, on signals from other circuits and feedback signals from their own circuit that influence their activity and performance.

Nerve signals make different things happen, whether it's moving an arm or talking, depending on the frequency and the timing with which they are sent, to what parts of the brain or body they are sent, and in what *combinations* they are sent.

What is a combination of nerve signals? Simply a certain grouping or coding of signals that allows the brain or nerves to do just one thing and only that one thing. It takes one combination, for example, for you to say "Good morning" and another combination—but of the same kind of signals—for a bird to chirp or a dog to bark. In a way, the signals are like musical notes that, in different combinations, play different melodies.

Where do combinations of nerve signals originate? Suppose you are about to say "Good morning." Some signals come from the thinking part of your brain, which is responsible for planning what you want to say. Other signals, of course, come from the speech area, where signals for words are assembled. The cerebellum and other parts of the brain concerned with the smooth action of muscles contribute signals that make you speak clearly, rather than in a jerky or slurred fashion. Memory circuits play a role too, because you obviously have to call on your memory to understand the meaning of words. Brain circuits concerned with emotion, finally, may add signals that lend zest to what you say so that you come forth with a cheerful "Good morning!" instead of a dismal grunt.

All these signals converge in the brain stem, where the nerves for the talking muscles begin. This, in extremely simple terms, illustrates how combinations of nerve signals do the work of the brain and nerves. These signals, which "speak" the same language in the same way for the nerve cells and nerves of all the creatures of the world, do seem to prove that, as it is written in Genesis, the whole earth, in a sense, really is of one language.

The spine is a series of bones running down your back. You sit on one end and your head sits on the other.

—ANONYMOUS

CHAPTER 7

The Cable in the Backbone

Racetrack fans are well aware that there are moments when all four legs of a galloping horse are off the ground at the same time. How does a horse manage to move with the speed, grace, and precision that enables it to do this? How is this superb timing accomplished? It is a function of the horse's *spinal cord*, as well as of its brain, just as the act of walking is accomplished by a person's spinal cord and brain.

The spinal cord is both a cable and a switchboard. As a cable, it connects the brain with the nerves of the body. As a switchboard, it coordinates muscle movements and other activities under its direct, local control.

The spinal cord is actually a taillike extension of the brain composed of the same kinds of nerve cells, nerve fibers, and supporting glial cells as those of the brain. It is also protected by the same three wrappings and the same fluid that cover the brain. It occupies a tunnel in the backbone that runs from the brain stem at the back of the head down to the level of the lowest, or twelfth, ribs. In the neck the human spinal cord is about as big around as a man's index finger. Below the neck it is smaller.

On each side of the cord, along its entire length, there are two rows of nerve fibers that merge as they pass from the spine out to the body and become nerves of the body (Figure 13). The hindmost row

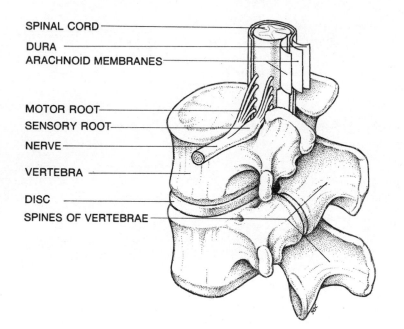

SPINAL CORD
DURA
ARACHNOID MEMBRANES

MOTOR ROOT
SENSORY ROOT

NERVE

VERTEBRA

DISC
SPINES OF VERTEBRAE

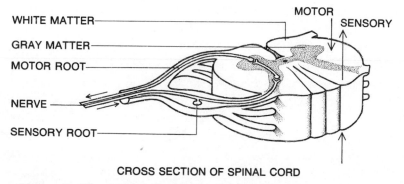

WHITE MATTER
GRAY MATTER
MOTOR ROOT

NERVE

SENSORY ROOT

MOTOR
SENSORY

CROSS SECTION OF SPINAL CORD

Figure 13. The spinal cord and one of its nerves.

consists of *sensory fibers,* which carry sensations from the body to the cord. The forward row consists of *motor fibers,* which emerge from the cord to conduct nerve signals to muscles and other parts of the body (Figure 13).

The nerve cells that exchange all the incoming and outgoing nerve signals of the cord are located in its center—in a core shaped like a butterfly—and make up its gray matter.

The nerve fibers that transmit nerve signals up and down the cord (indicated by arrows in Figure 13) form part of its white matter.

As an illustration of how the wiring system of the cord works, let's consider its role in walking.

Suppose you start walking by stepping forward with your right leg. Several things have to happen—all at the same time. As muscles on the front of the leg lift it, muscles on the back of the leg have to relax or go limp. Meanwhile, muscles that keep the left leg steady have to contract in order to keep you from falling. Nerve cells in the lower part of the cord see to it that these different sets of muscles do their jobs smoothly, with perfect timing, and continue to do so as you keep walking. Were it not for perfect timing, you would stumble or drop to the ground.

Perfect timing depends on a constant flow, from the leg muscles, of nerve signals that keep the spinal cord informed of the changing positions of the legs, so that nerve cells in the cord will move the legs in the proper sequence. This is known as a *feedback system,* of which there are hundreds throughout the body's nervous system.

When we walk, portions of the brain concerned with leg movements are constantly receiving and sending nerve signals to control the direction and speed of walking. These signals between the cord and the brain are transmitted by the long up-and-down nerve fibers in the white matter of the spinal cord—its wiring system.

Knowledge of the cord's wiring system is essential for interpreting diagnostic tests that show whether anything is wrong with the spinal cord or its nerves. A diagnostic test with which we are all familiar is the knee-jerk, or reflex, test.

When a doctor taps the tendon in the front of your knee, the tendon is pressed enough to send signals to the spinal cord. These signals are immediately relayed from the back portion of the cord's gray matter to nerve cells in the front of the gray matter. The latter are the cells that make the thigh muscles contract and kick the leg out.

If the leg does not budge when the knee is tapped, this suggests that there may be something wrong with the "kick" nerves or with the section of the spinal cord that controls them. Such trouble could be caused by nerve injury, pressure from a slipped disc, or some other kind of ailment.

If the leg kicks out wildly and violently, on the other hand, it could be a symptom of trouble higher up in the spinal cord or even in the brain—trouble that is interfering with the brain's control over the lower portion of the spinal cord. The trouble might be a disease like multiple sclerosis or a tumor or injury affecting the spinal cord or brain.

In either case, the doctor would perform other tests to pinpoint the exact location and nature of any trouble. These include tests of other reflexes, tests of muscle power, and tests to find out whether and where there is any numbness of the skin or loss of any other kind of sensation. Finally, special tests, such as X rays and scan tests, are usually called for, to make certain of the exact location and nature of the trouble.

All our perceptions are dependent on . . . our nerves.

—DAVID HUME,
Scottish philosopher, 1711–1776.

CHAPTER 8

Nerves:
The Wiring System of the
Body

How does information from the body and from the world around us reach the brain? How does the brain send messages to the muscles, glands, and other parts of the body, to put them to work? By nerves—the wiring system of the body.

There are three sets of nerves: nerves of the brain, called *cranial nerves;* nerves of the body, called *spinal,* or *peripheral, nerves;* and nerves of the autonomic, or "automatic," system.

A nerve is simply a bundle of nerve fibers, located outside the brain and spinal cord, enclosed in a sleeve of tissue. There are no nerves inside the brain or spinal cord.

Nerves are round, glistening, and flexible. They may be short and slender, like those of the eye muscles; or long and thick, like the sciatic nerves of the legs. Most nerves split off into smaller and smaller branches on their course to remote parts of the body. As a result of all this branching and rebranching, there are hundreds of nerves in the body.

Most nerves are composed of nerve fibers that send information *to* the brain or spinal cord, and of other nerve fibers that send signals *from* the brain or spinal cord. They are *mixed nerves.* Nerves like those concerned with seeing and hearing, which are made up almost entirely of nerve fibers concerned with sensations, are *sensory nerves.* Nerves like those that make the eyes move are made up almost entirely of nerve fibers that control mechanical action. They are *motor* nerves. Almost all nerves include nerve fibers of the *autonomic nervous system* (ANS).

The autonomic nervous system is a vast network of nerve-cell clusters, called ganglia, and their connecting nerves. The largest part of this system is located in front of the vertebrae along their entire length. The solar plexus, which is behind the stomach, is part of the network.

The autonomic system is a dual system consisting of *sympathetic* and *parasympathetic* nerves (Lennart Heimer, neuroanatomist). Most, but not all, of the sympathetic nerves speed up bodily activities; most of the parasympathetic nerves slow them down.

This dual action is especially important in emergencies, for it shuts down activities that are not essential at the moment, while speeding up bodily functions that are necessary to cope with the emergency.

Suppose, for instance, that an animal or person suddenly must fight or flee from an enemy. The muscles in his limbs will then need extra blood, but his stomach and intestines will not need as much as they usually do. To guarantee an ample supply of blood to the muscles, the sympathetic nerves shut down the amount of blood sent to the stomach and intestines so that blood in their arteries can be safely shunted to the muscles. At the same time the sympathetic system sees to it that the flow of blood through the muscles is as rich and powerful as it can possibly be. The sympathetic nerves do this by speeding up the heart and by raising the blood pressure.

The blood pressure, incidentally, is also regulated by a hormone the heart secretes. The hormone, produced by cells around its major openings, adjusts the blood pressure by altering the caliber of body arteries and the output of fluid by the kidneys. The heart is therefore an endocrine gland as well as a pump.

Nerves of the autonomic system have many other functions. They control the tear glands, the size of the pupils and the shape of the lenses, the blanching or blushing of the skin, and, as noted in Chapter 3, body temperature. (Obviously, this system plays a role in emotional responses.)

You can't see or feel nerves the way you can see and feel tendons like those in the back of your hands or behind your knees. Nerves are too well hidden under the skin and muscles. The only nerves that can be seen without being exposed by surgery are the ends of the optic nerves at the back of each eyeball. To see them a doctor needs a special instrument, an ophthalmoscope, which enables him to see the interior of the eye and inspect the retina, its blood vessels, and the forward end of the optic nerve at the back of the eye.

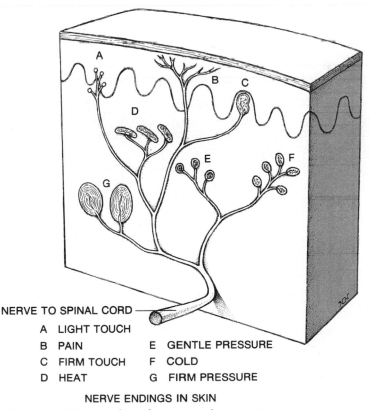

NERVE TO SPINAL CORD

A LIGHT TOUCH
B PAIN   E GENTLE PRESSURE
C FIRM TOUCH   F COLD
D HEAT   G FIRM PRESSURE

NERVE ENDINGS IN SKIN

Figure 14. Nerve endings for various skin sensations.

One nerve of which you may sometimes become painfully aware is your "funny bone" nerve. It is so close to the skin, at the inner side of your elbow, that it can easily get banged. It is not the bang on the bone, the ulna, but the bang on the elbow nerve, the ulnar nerve, that causes the temporary sharp waves of pain. These waves are really a series of electric shocks. Since nerves are charged with a small electrical current, a bang on one of them can initiate abrupt changes in the electrical charge, resulting in unnatural, or "funny," nerve signals that feel like shocks because they actually are shocks!

How do the skin and other parts of the body pick up news of the neighborhood? Either by the bare ends of sensory nerve fibers or by terminals of nerve fibers called *end organs*. End organs are somewhat larger than nerve cells and have different shapes, depending on what kind of sensation they detect.

Some end organs in the skin let you know when and where it has been touched lightly, and others when and where it has been touched more firmly. There are also special end organs in the skin for the detection of pain, cold, warmth, light pressure, and heavy pressure. The signals from the end organs are transmitted toward the spinal cord by nerve fibers that become part of a nerve (Figure 14).

Just about all parts of the body as well as the skin have special end organs or special cells for picking up information. Muscles have cells that indicate their *position* so that you know, without looking, whether your arm is straight or bent. Joints have *pain* detectors, as anyone knows who has suffered from arthritis or a sprained ankle. And the stomach and intestines are rich in special cells that sense the arrival of food, start the reflexes that pour out digestive juices, churn the food, send it on its way, and inform you of hunger or pain.

In addition, the nose, eyes, ears, mouth, tongue, and throat each have their own special cells for getting news of the neighborhood. And each kind of cell does only the job it is supposed to do. A seeing cell in the eye, for example, cannot tell hot from cold any more than a skin cell can see.

Information detected by the nose, eyes, ears, and other parts of the head is sent directly to the brain by the *cranial nerves*. There are twenty-four of them, twelve on each side, known by the numbers and names shown in Table 1. All of them are *under* the brain, as indicated in Figure 17.

The olfactory, or first cranial, nerve, for the sense of smell, and the optic, or second cranial, nerve, for vision, enter the undersurface of the cerebral hemispheres. The other cranial nerves, ten on each side, are connected to the brain stem (Figure 22).

The next four chapters consider functions of the cranial nerves in detail.

Table 1
THE CRANIAL NERVES

Number	Function	Technical Names
1	Smelling	Olfactory nerve
2	Seeing	Optic nerve
3	Moving eyeball	Oculomotor nerve
4	Rotating eyeball slightly	Trochlear, or pulley, nerve
5	Sensation of face and eye; moving the jaw and chewing	Trigeminal, the three part nerve
6	Moving eye outward	Abducens nerve
7	Moving face muscles, as in smiling and talking	Facial nerve
8	a. Hearing b. Balance/Dizziness	Cochlea, or "sea-shell," nerve Vestibular nerve
9	Throat sensation and swallowing muscles	Glossopharyngeal nerve, the swallowing and throat nerve
10	Mostly for voice, heart, stomach, and gut control	Vagus, or "wandering," nerve, because it is so far-reaching
11	Moving shoulder and neck muscles, as in shrugging	Spinal Accessory nerve
12	Moving the tongue	Hypoglossal, or "under-the-tongue," nerve

*". . . from a long and distant past . . . the smell and taste of things remain
. . . bearing in the tiny and almost impalpable drop of their essence the vast
structure of recollection."*

—MARCEL PROUST
Swann's Way, Remembrance of Things Past

CHAPTER 9

How Your Nose Knows

The quotation from *Swann's Way* refers to the smell and taste of
a madeleine given to Marcel by his aunt. This madeleine is possibly the
most famous small cake in literature. It summoned up for Proust a past
that he felt could be recaptured and relived if recreated in a work of
art. Certainly you, too, have memories that can be suddenly evoked by
a particular smell or taste, which seems to have a sentimental and
aesthetic value all its own.

Yet the sense of smell is of minor importance to modern man—
whereas the life of lower animals depends on it. They use it to forage
for food and to warn themselves of the danger of an approaching
predator. It is also important to them for sex recognition and sexual
stimulation—in contrast to the much feebler role it plays, in these two
respects, in humans. The perfume industry, however, recognizes and
exploits the attraction that certain scents do have for us.

Proust intuitively realized that the senses of smell and taste are
intimately related. We, too, are aware of this. When we have a bad
head cold and a stuffy nose, we not only lose our sense of smell, but

often find that our food is tasteless. This is because the centers for taste and smell are located close together in the brain and are interdependent.

Primitive man probably had a more highly developed sense of smell than we do, because, like animals, he needed it to survive. But ours is still useful. If we smell smoke, we worry about fire and look for its cause—or get out of the house in a hurry. If we smell a skunk, we move quickly away. If the meat smells bad, we throw it out rather than risk food poisoning. And there are certain rotten odors that we associate with putrefaction or disease, situations to be avoided because of the risk of infection or contamination. So our sense of smell still works to protect us to a certain extent.

How do we actually smell "smells"? Odors, whether good or bad, are carried into the nose by invisible airborne chemicals (Figure 15).

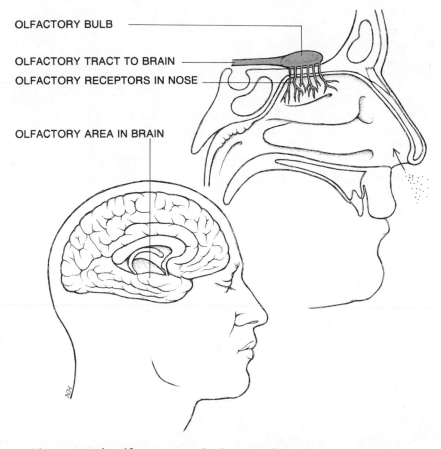

OLFACTORY BULB

OLFACTORY TRACT TO BRAIN

OLFACTORY RECEPTORS IN NOSE

OLFACTORY AREA IN BRAIN

Figure 15. The olfactory tract, the first cranial nerve.

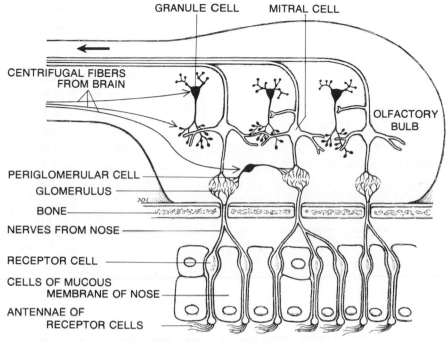

Figure 16. Processing cells of the olfactory bulb.

These are dissolved in the moisture of the nose to form a chemical solution. The chemical solution then stimulates minute hairlike "antennae" that extend a short distance into the upper part of the nose from very small nerve cells called *receptor cells.* Millions of these cells are sandwiched in between the cells of the mucous membrane of the nose (Figure 16). Dr. Lewis Thomas, physician and author, has called attention to an unusual feature of the receptor cells. The life span of these cells is only about three weeks, after which they whither and die, and are replaced by new ones. They are the *only* nerve cells in the body that are replaced. All others that are destroyed by injury, disease, or age are never replaced.

The receptor cells translate information from the antennae into electrochemical impulses or nerve signals, after which they pass these signals through short, slender nerves to two structures inside the head—the right and left *olfactory bulbs.*

The olfactory bulbs are each roughly the size and shape of a small lima bean and are located above the nose. The nerves from the nose reach them after passing through tiny apertures in the bone covering the nose.

You have not yet smelled the smell, and you won't until messages from the bulbs have been sent to the brain and interpreted there. Before signals of smell are sent to the brain, they have to be sorted and coded in the bulbs.

This process is carried out by rounded structures called *glomeruli,* and by nerve cells above them called *mitral cells* (because they have a triangular shape like a bishop's mitre; see Figure 16). The mitral cells are the last stop for signals headed for the brain. The other nerve cells in the bulbs modulate the processing of signals by inhibiting or activating the mitral cells and the glomeruli. They do this fine-tuning, in less than a second, via thousands of interconnecting synapses.

Processed olfactory messages travel to the brain through the two olfactory tracts, one for each olfactory bulb. Each tract is about an inch and a half long and behaves like a nerve, although it is actually an extension of the brain and not truly a nerve. Early anatomists did think it was a nerve and therefore called it the first cranial nerve, a term that has persisted.

Each olfactory tract winds up on the undersurface of the brain, where some of its nerve fibers enter a section of the frontal lobe and others the temporal lobe. The innermost portion of each temporal lobe's cortex registers and interprets the signals it receives in a way that tells you have smelled an odor and what it is. Finally!

Nearby areas of the cortex help interpret olfactory signals and help you decide what, if anything, you should do about the odor you have finally smelled.

Cortical areas for the sense of smell are connected to the hippocampus, which has a role in our remembrance of scents and "things past"; to the *amygdala,* which influences emotional reactions to odors; and to the hypothalamus, which controls the autonomic nervous system and the activity of the sex glands (Figure 10). These connections explain why there is more to the sense of smell than simply the detection of odors.

The deep structures just listed, incidentally, are all part of the "old" primitive portion of the brain known as the limbic brain, which I'll discuss in Chapter 13. This is not surprising, for the sense of smell is a primitive sensation and one of the first an infant animal experiences. It has to rely on this sense while it is unable to see, to locate the source of its mother's milk.

A great deal of research has been and continues to be devoted to the sense of smell in animals, largely because of its association with these deep primitive areas of the limbic brain in man as well as in animals.

Animal studies, it has been hoped, would show how equivalent parts of the human brain function and are "wired."

There are two broad aspects related to studies of the sense of smell in animals: (1) observation of the effects of scents on behavior, and (2) methods of tracing and then mapping the olfactory wiring system from the nose to the brain.

Extensive studies of the sense of smell in rats, mice, and other animals have been described by Richard L. Doty, neurophysiologist, and colleagues, in his book on mammalian olfaction. These studies show that animals deprived of the sense of smell are subject to various kinds of sexual disturbances.

For example, young female rats that can smell and see a mature male rat develop sexually more rapidly than females that see but cannot smell the male rat. The females that can smell a male have more frequent estrous cycles, their sex glands become larger, and their interest in the sex act becomes noticeably more enthusiastic than in rats deprived of the sense of smell. The deprived rats, in fact, tend to be appreciably slow to mature.

Loss of smell in sexually naive male rats actually abolishes their mating ability; and in mature rats these instincts are dulled. Odors can also affect the social behavior of male rats. The smell of a rival or a strange rat can lead to violent aggression.

How have the brain's pathways for olfaction been identified and mapped? The methods are the same as those which have been used to study other brain circuits, so we shall review them briefly.

The first identifications of olfactory and other brain connections were originally made through dissection and inspection by the naked eye. Detailed knowledge became possible only about one hundred years ago, thanks to two major discoveries. One was that nerve cells and their connecting nerve fibers could be detected under the microscope, in exquisite detail, when stained with various gold, silver, or other chemical compounds. The other major discovery was that the locations, connections, and functions of different parts of the brain could be identified by electrical means.

Different stains reveal different characteristics of nerve cells and their axons and dendrites. One special stain shows neurons that have withered or died after their axons have been cut.

Conversely, another stain reveals axons that have withered after their nerve cells have been destroyed. These stains indicate the *course* of conducting pathways in the brain. And there are fluorescent stains that literally light up axons, when viewed through a microscope, thus revealing their course through the brain.

Another investigative strategy involves the use of mildly radioactive substances that can be detected in various ways after they have settled in nerve cells. Neurons, for example, gobble up sugar in the form of glucose. By injecting into the bloodstream a form of glucose which has been radioactively "tagged," researchers can load neurons with this unusual substance. Since the neurons can't distinguish it from ordinary glucose, they pick it right up. Then, when stimulated by nerve signals sent from remote parts of the brain, these neurons react differently from others nearby that have not been stimulated. This technique has proved to be particularly valuable for identifying neurons in the visual cortex that respond only to certain kinds of images flashed in front of the eyes.

Other methods of studying details of nerve cells include special stains that outline tiny, vital structures within them, and the use of the electron microscope, which magnifies images to 125,000 times their natural size or more.

There are two kinds of electrical methods for mapping brain circuits: electrical stimulation and electrical recording. Electrical stimulation can supply clues as to the functions of given parts of the brain. If you stimulate a certain area, does it result in the twitching of an arm or leg? If you stimulate another area, does the subject fly into a rage? And does stimulation of still another area result in the production of an unusually large amount of sex hormones in the blood?

Electrical recording can also be used to trace conducting pathways and their destinations. By introducing a number of fine recording electrodes into the brain and observing which of them reveals changes in the electrical pattern when other parts of the brain are stimulated, one can pinpoint the precise location of a pathway and its destination. There are even some microelectrodes that are so small they can be introduced into a single tiny nerve cell to record (or stimulate) activity within it. This, in highly simplified form, is how scientists have identified and mapped the pathways, cell clusters, and general areas of the brain.

When applied to studies of the sense of smell, such techniques have shown that structures in the olfactory bulb are electrically active at all times, and that natural animal scents and artificial chemical odors alter this electrical activity in fairly specific ways. These kinds of tests have also disclosed areas on the surface of the brain, and deep within it, that comprise parts of the olfactory circuits.

One of the most interesting discoveries to date is that electrical stimulation of an olfactory bulb in a male rat activates cells in the hypothalamus, deep in the forward part of the brain (Figure 10), resulting in the production of the male sex hormone called *gonadotropin*. The scent of a female rat is known to increase the production of gonadotropin, presumably by activation of the same olfactory bulb and hypothalamic circuit. Gonadotropin plays a significant role in arousing the sexual interest and behavior of male rats. This experiment shows how a specific odor can influence the production of a sex hormone.

Conversely, injections of male sex hormones increase, or "jazz up," electrical activity in parts of the hypothalamus and parts of the brain having to do with the sense of smell. Such tests clearly show that: (1) sex hormones can affect olfactory circuits, (2) olfactory circuits can alter hormone production. This also applies, in principle, to female rats and animals of other species. As a result of these observations we may, in time, find out more about similar circuits in the human brain.

Let us now turn to clinical aspects of the sense of smell. When performing surgery, I have occasionally had to cut both olfactory tracts in order to seal an enlarged artery (aneurysm) at the base of the brain (Figure 26a). This, of course, made it impossible for such patients to smell their food or taste it properly. They were like people with a bad head cold. Their sense of taste was not entirely lost, because the taste buds of the tongue, connected to the brain through the ninth cranial nerve, remained intact. But the taste buds alone are not sufficient to give a full sense of the flavor of food.

And although these people could not smell, they could tell when an irritating substance like ammonia entered the nose. Ammonia irritates nerve endings of the fifth cranial nerve, which detects this kind of sensation, as well as detecting sensations of the face and controlling the jaw muscles.

We noted earlier that the reason the senses of smell and taste are intimately connected is because their end stations in the brain are close to each other. This undoubtedly has evolutionary significance. The first animals to have even a tiny primitive brain obviously depended on both smell and taste to know what they should or should not eat.

Finally, people suffering from a brain tumor or scar deep in the brain, in the region of the olfactory and taste areas, often have peculiar epileptic spells in which they make smacking movements of the mouth as if they were tasting something, and complain of smelling an odor— often like burning rubber. Fortunately, a neurosurgeon can usually cure these patients by removing the offending tumor or scar.

The light of the body is the eye.
—MATTHEW 6:22

CHAPTER 10

The Windows of the Brain

What you see, like what you smell, is processed outside the brain itself before it is finally recorded and interpreted there. In this case, the eyes do the initial processing. *Photons* of light, which make up the images of what you see, are translated by the retina into nerve signals. The signals are then processed by the retina, which, like the olfactory bulb, serves as a minicomputer. It sorts and codes signals, and amplifies or reduces them, to ready them for transmission to the brain. It's a complex process that can't be described "in a nutshell."

Let's start at the beginning, with *your* eyes. Are they blue, brown, or hazel? That depends on the color of the *iris,* which is the eye's circular shutter; in fact, it behaves just like the shutter in a camera. The black hole in its center, the *pupil,* corresponds to the aperture of a camera. The size of the pupil changes constantly, automatically adjusted by delicate muscles. They are controlled by nerves of the autonomic system, which functions whether you want it to or not.

If you are standing in a dim light, the pupils of your eyes will be wide open, to let in as much light as possible. In a very bright light, the pupils close down almost completely, automatically saving you from being blinded by the glare.

The lens of each eye has much the same function and shape as a camera's lens. It is about the size of a small seedless grape and is filled with a clear jellylike substance. Because it is not solid, like a glass lens, its shape can be adjusted to sharpen the focus of images. Thin muscle strands pull its edges outward to flatten the lens. Relaxation of the muscles allows the lens to become thicker, thus readjusting the focus.

In addition to its role in focusing images, each lens, like a camera lens, transfers images from right to left, and vice versa, as light passes through it. This means that the left half of the *retina* (the inner lining) receives images coming from the right side of the eye and that the right half of each retina receives images from the left side (Figure 17). The *left* half of *each* retina communicates these images, by nerve signals, to the *left* vision area of the brain, and vice versa. This is because of the way the optic, or seeing, nerves are arranged. So everything we see to our right is registered in the left side of our brain, and everything we see to our left is registered in the right side. Damage to the right visual area of the brain will, therefore, result in blindness to everything to the left of the body, and vice versa.

The "lens cap" is a clear sturdy layer of tissue called the *cornea*. It is the windshield of the eye, and like the windshield of an automobile, it has wipers, the eyelids, and fluid to wash it. The fluid is produced by the *tear gland,* located above each eye (which, like the iris and the lens, is controlled by autonomic nerves) and is dispensed by the tear duct, the pinkish tissue visible at the inside of each eye. Sensitive nerve ends in the cornea, from the fifth cranial nerve, let you know when you have a painful speck in your eye.

The position of each eye is adjusted by five straplike muscles. They allow you to look up, down, to one side or the other, and help you focus images by making the eyes converge when looking at objects very close up. One muscle pulls the eye down, another up, while the third moves the eye inward toward the nose. These muscles are controlled by the *oculomotor,* or third cranial, nerve (Figure 18). A fourth muscle, smaller than the others, runs through a pulleylike loop of tissue above each eye to rotate the eyeball slightly. It is operated by the *trochlear* (Latin for "pulley"), or fourth cranial nerve. The muscle that pulls the eye outward, or "leads it away," is controlled by the abdu-

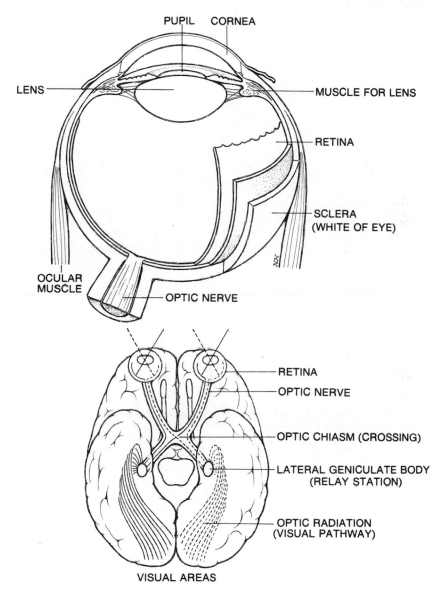

PUPIL   CORNEA

LENS

MUSCLE FOR LENS

RETINA

SCLERA
(WHITE OF EYE)

OCULAR
MUSCLE

OPTIC NERVE

RETINA

OPTIC NERVE

OPTIC CHIASM (CROSSING)

LATERAL GENICULATE BODY
(RELAY STATION)

OPTIC RADIATION
(VISUAL PATHWAY)

VISUAL AREAS

Figure 17. The eye, and the visual pathways in the brain.

cens, or sixth cranial nerve. The trigeminal, or fifth cranial nerve, as
mentioned above, is responsible for sensations of pain in the eye. Finally, the eyelids are controlled by branches of the facial, or seventh
cranial nerve. A slender autonomic nerve alters the size of the pupil,

NERVES OF THE EYE

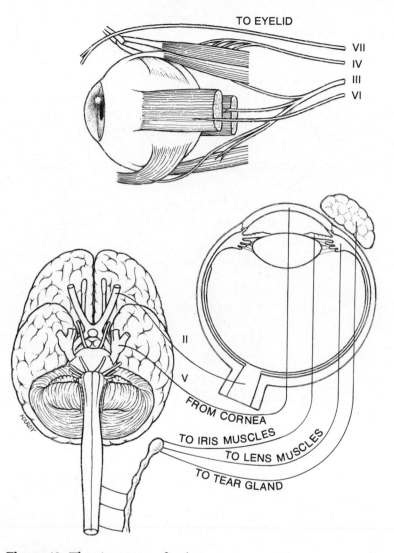

Figure 18. The nine nerves of each eye:
II. Optic, or second cranial nerve, for vision.
III, IV, VI: The third, fourth, and sixth cranial nerves, for moving the
eyeball.
V. The fifth cranial nerve, for corneal sensation.
VII. The seventh (facial) nerve, for moving the eyelids.
The three autonomic (automatic) nerves, for the iris, lens, and tear
gland.

another adjusts the shape of the lens, and a third activates the tear gland, which keeps the outer surface of the eye moist.

An extraordinary thing about the movement of the eyes is that they constantly shift very slightly to and fro, at the rate of five times a second, without our knowing it, as Barlow and Molton have pointed out. This automatic scanning mechanism is apparently necessary for sharpness of vision. Whether we like it or not, all of us are literally "shifty-eyed." In addition to these waking movements, our eyes wander rapidly and randomly in a certain stage of our sleep. This is known as the REM (rapid *eye* *movement*) stage of sleep. The pattern of these rapid random movements changes as we dream.

The jellylike substance, the vitreous, inside each eyeball keeps it from collapsing. Without this substance, the eyeball would deflate like a football with the air let out. There is also a small compartment filled with clear fluid in front of the iris of each eye, to protect it somewhat.

The retina, which is the inner lining of the eyeball, is composed of several layers of cells. Pigment cells form its innermost layer (Figure 19). This pigment layer gives the human retina its red color, which explains why a person's eyes looks red in flash photographs. (A dog's eyes, however, shine with a yellow glare and a deer's with a whitish gleam when reflecting a bright light at night.)

Immediately in front of the pigment layer there is a layer of 125 million *rods* and *cones*. They are known as *photoreceptor cells* because they respond to light. The cones, most of which are concentrated around the optic nerve at the back of the eye, are mainly responsible for sharpness of vision and for the detection of colors. They are also principally concerned with straight-ahead, central vision.

Most of the rods are located farther from the optic nerve, at the very back of the eyeball, than the cones. They are therefore in an ideal position to pick up images that are passed through the lens from objects that are seen off to one side. The rods, in a word, are the cells that enable us to see "out of the corner of our eyes." This is known as *peripheral vision*. Although the rods do not detect colors, they are able to detect images in a dim light, which the cones cannot do. So rods are also the cells that allow us to see at night.

Both the rods and the cones translate what they "see" into nerve signals that are flashed to cells in front of them called *ganglion cells*. The ganglion cells (Figure 19) then transmit the signals for vision to the brain, by way of the optic nerves.

Matters are not quite that simple, however, because there are

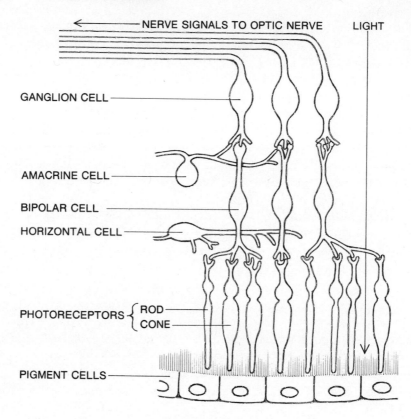

Figure 19. Retinal cells, for the initial processing of vision.

nerve cells between the receptor cells and the ganglion cells that share in the complicated coding and modulation of nerve signals which take place in the retina. They are the amacrine and horizontal cells shown in Figure 19.

The coding system analyzes and distinguishes fixed, moving, vertical, and horizontal lines, as well as colors, and most other aspects of things seen. The retina, thin as it is, performs a stupendous amount of highly complicated work. Science writer Jeanne McDermott explains that "our retina, which has maybe 125 million rods and cones as well as four other types of specialized cells, performs the equivalent of 10 billion calculations per second." In contrast to this, she continues, "a good personal computer can perform only about eight million calculations per second." Think of it—10 billion calculations in the retina before the brain or you know what your eyes have seen!

Nerve signals from the retina reach the brain by way of the optic nerves. These nerves are composed of nerve fibers that are the axons, or "sending fibers," of ganglion cells. There are about one million axons in each optic nerve.

Where in the brain do the axons of the optic nerves end up? Half of them from each eye cross over, as indicated in Figure 17, to the opposite side of the brain. They are first received by clusters of nerve cells in the brain stem—two clusters on each side.

These stations of cells relay some signals from the eyes *directly* up to the vision area above them, and relay other signals to the vision area through parts of the basal ganglia (described in Chapter 3). The brain-stem relay stations also have two-way communications with the cortex (above them) and the retina (in front of them) that take care of the automatic focusing of the eyes. That is, they help control the eye movements and adjustments of the lenses that are necessary for sharp focus.

The brain informs us of what we see by means of the two vision areas, located at the back of the brain (Figure 6). The nerve cells of the *left* vision area are arranged so that they form a detailed map of every-thing the *left* half of *each* retina sees, and vice versa. Some of these nerve cells react only to horizontal lines detected by the retina, others only to vertical lines, and still others only to moving lines or to corners, as discovered by David H. Hubel, neurobiologist. There are also cells for recognizing color, and, apparently, cells for giving us stereo (in-depth) vision.

Like a computer, the vision areas of the brain speedily put all this information together to give us a mental picture of what we see, and then relay the information to other parts of the brain. Information concerning words we read, for example, is relayed from the vision areas to the speech area, which interprets the meaning of those words. Infor-mation about an approaching automobile is relayed to the motor areas so that we can step aside.

Information concerning what we see is also sent to deep parts of the brain, such as the almond-shaped structure known as the amygdala, close to the hippocampus shown in Figure 23. They share in the pro-cessing of emotional responses and memories related to scenes and sights.

Scientists have mapped the anatomy of all these and other parts of the brain concerned with the sense of vision, and their functions have been discovered by combinations of the investigative strategies de-scribed in Chapter 9.

What about clinical problems of vision, such as double vision, partial blindness, imaginary images, and the flashing zigzag lines that some people see? What causes these disorders—and, to begin with, how are functions of the eyes tested? Eye tests are extremely important not only for the medical influence they may have on vision, but also because they can reveal a great deal about a host of other afflictions ranging from diabetes and arteriosclerosis to brain tumors and drug addiction.

If the person tested has pupils that are almost as small as pinpoints, this could be due to the use of such powerful drugs as morphine, codein, and cocaine. Is just one pupil exceptionally large? This suggests pressure on the pupil's nerve, the nerve of the iris, by a tumor or blood clot inside the head.

Do the eyes track normally? If not, a person will see double, perhaps because of pressure affecting nerves of one or more of the eye muscles. Can the person move his eyes in an upward direction? If he cannot do so, this is usually a sign of trouble with part of the automatic focusing system in the brain stem. A common cause of this trouble is pressure from a tumor on the pineal gland, located immediately above the brain stem.

Do the eyes move jerkily and rapidly to and fro when a person is asked to look to his extreme right or left? If they do, this is generally a sign of trouble in a part of the ear or brain that controls muscle coordination and balance.

If a person is partially blind, there are tests that can determine where the source of trouble is. If he cannot see at all with one eye, the trouble is in that eye or its optic nerve. If he cannot see toward the left with either eye, this points to trouble in the right side of the brain, where all signals for left-sided vision wind up. And if he cannot see anything toward the left with his left eye, nor anything to the right with his right eye, this indicates pressure on the optic nerves where half of their fibers cross over (this area is called *optic chiasm*). As Figure 17 indicates, the fibers that cross are in the middle of this crossing. They serve the nasal half of each retina. The nasal half of the left retina sees only to the left, and the nasal half of the right retina sees only to the right. This kind of visual field defect can be accurately detected and mapped on a special chart by appropriate testing of the range of vision. A tumor on the pituitary gland (which is under the chiasm) is the most frequent cause of this kind of disturbance.

Inspection of the interior of each eye with an ophthalmoscope is an essential part of eye testing. In this way, a doctor can look at the optic nerve and blood vessels around it. If the nerve looks as white as a sheet, this means serious and often permanent damage to the nerve, either from nerve disease or from pressure on the nerve inside the head. If the nerve looks swollen and congested, this suggests pressure inside the head from a brain tumor.

Arteries that are very thin and shiny are characteristic of high blood pressure. Arteries that look kinked and chalky are typical of arteriosclerosis. Tiny hemorrhages and small deposits of grayish white matter in the retina, depending on their nature, are suggestive of diabetes or serious kidney disease.

What about other clinical aspects of vision? Attacks of migraine are commonly accompanied by an excruciating headache on one side of the head and temporary blindness to everything toward the opposite side of the nose. In addition, flashing zigzag lines generally keep darting hither and yon in the blinded field of vision. It seems clear that such attacks temporarily upset the left visual pathways somewhere along their course between the eyes and the back of the brain. I believe that severe spasms of brain arteries are the cause of this pain and visual disturbance.

Visual hallucinations are another (though rare) symptom of trouble in brain pathways related to vision. People with a scar or tumor in a part of a temporal lobe that is close to visual pathways may suffer epileptic spells ushered in by imaginary scenes. And some of my patients, after I had removed a large benign brain tumor that had been pressing on one of the vision areas at the back of their head, complained for a day or two of seeing animals crawling on the ceiling of their hospital room. When their visual cortex began functioning normally, these hallucinations no longer occurred.

To sum up, the eyes have it—the ability of a camera to "take pictures" and the ability of a space satellite to translate relayed images into coded signals that are converted into pictures.

He that hath ears to hear, let him hear.
—MATTHEW 11:15

CHAPTER 11

Your Snail-Shell and Balance Nerves

Escargots, a treat to some palates including mine, dwell, of course, in snail shells. Cousins of these snail shells dwell inside part of the human ear. They are small bony structures with spiral coils exactly like those of an escargot's shell. This "snail shell" in each of our ears is called the *cochlea,* Latin for "shell" (whence comes the English word cockle in the nursery rhyme "Mary, Mary, Quite Contrary"). Its job is to translate vibrations of sound into nerve signals and flash them to the brain via the *cochlear nerve.* Known also as the *auditory* or *acoustic nerve,* it comprises one half of the ear nerve, the eighth cranial nerve (Table 1). The other half of the eighth nerve, described later, is the *balance,* or *vestibular, nerve.*

Sounds, as we all know, travel through air. They can also travel through water, earth, and bone. Whales and dolphins rely on waterborne sounds for communication. We, too, can hear when underwater and thus, for example, recognize the sound of an approaching motorboat. By putting an ear to the ground, we can also hear sounds that have traveled through the earth, just as the scouts and Indians of the Old West did when listening for the sounds of distant hoofbeats. In addition, we can hear sounds transmitted by the bones of the skull. Press a vibrating tuning fork anywhere against your head and you can hear its sound. Doctors use the tuning fork in this manner as one of their tests for hearing.

Hearing is a complex process involving the delicate machinery of the ear, which includes three adjustable membranes, three movable bones, and ten thousand intricately constructed receptor organs.

Sounds are first detected by the *eardrum,* also called the *tympanic membrane.* It is not flat like a drumhead, but conical. The cone points inward from the outer part of the ear. The tension of the eardrum is adjusted by tiny muscles that, in a sense, are equivalent to the knobs of a kettle drum with which the tympanist of a symphony orchestra adjusts the tension of his instrument.

When the waves or vibrations of a sound enter the outer part of our ears, regardless of whether that sound is a word, a whisper, or a bang, they beat against our eardrums and jar them just as ocean waves beat against the side of a boat and jar it.

The vibrations of sound that jar an eardrum are passed on to a chain of three little jointed bones inside the drum. These movable bones are nested in a small cave filled with air. This air has reached the cave by way of a narrow passageway inside the head called the Eustachian tube, which originates at the back of the nose (Figure 20). In other words, the air in the cave is air you have breathed in through your nose.

The pressure of the air inside the cave has to be the same as the air pressure outside the drum if you are to hear properly. Sometimes, however, the Eustachian tube does not adjust the air pressure inside the eardrum quickly enough. Then you may hear a click in your ear, feel a little deaf, and even have an earache. This may have happened to you in an elevator or airplane that has gone up or down faster than your ear could adjust to the changing air pressure.

The first of the three little bones inside the air cave is the *hammer,* which is attached to the underneath inner surface of the eardrum. When the eardrum is jiggled by the vibrations of a sound, the *hammer* is jiggled in exactly the same way. It then jiggles the next bone, the

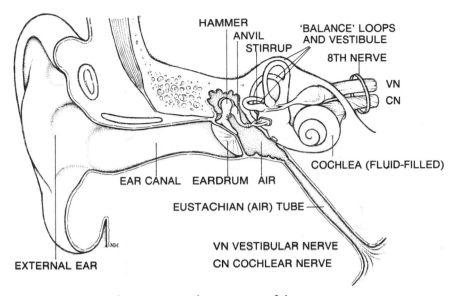

Figure 20. The anatomy and two nerves of the ear.

anvil, which in turn jiggles the third bone, the *stirrup.* (Does all this remind you of the old song "Dem Bones"?)

The stirrup is attached to a second and flexible membrane, sort of an inner eardrum, that forms a wall between the air cave and a second cave filled with fluid. This ear fluid is filtered from blood vessels and fills a part of the inner cave called the *vestibule.* Fluid also fills the coils of the cochlea and three loops of bone that help control balance.

When the stirrup makes this inner second membrane vibrate, the vibrations from it pass through the ear fluid into the coils of the cochlea. The vibrations then fetch up against a delicate membrane that stretches across the coils of the cochlea like the line across the letter Ø. This is the third flexible membrane of the ear. It is called the *basilar membrane* because there are thousands of tiny structures based on it that detect the vibrations and translate them into nerve signals for hearing.

The coils of each cochlea are also lined with about ten thousand of these structures. They were first described in fine detail by the Italian anatomist Alfonso Corti in the 1800s and are therefore known as the *organs of Corti.* A highly schematic diagram (Figure 21) illustrates their principle features.

As the diagram indicates, the rod-shaped body of this organ (in fact called a *rod*) sits on the basilar membrane, which is bathed by the

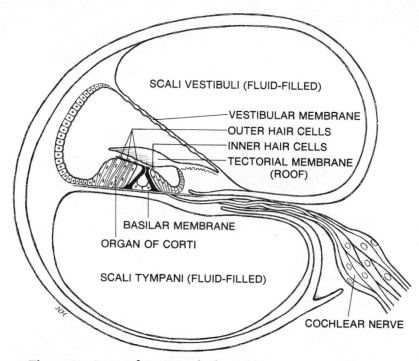

Figure 21. Organ of Corti, inside the cochlea.

ear fluid outside it. The other end of each rod has twenty short, stiff, hairlike *cilia*, which are held in place by a fixed rigid membrane above them called the *roof*, or *tectal membrane*. Each rod responds only to a certain frequency of signals. In this way, the ear sorts out high tones from low tones and interprets the pitch of various sounds.

The rods are stimulated in a complicated manner. The vibrations that have passed through the ear fluid, as described above, jiggle parts of the basilar membrane just enough to move the rod or rods sitting on that part of the membrane. This slight motion of a rod causes its stiff cilia to brush against, or "scratch," the rigid roof over them. The scratching action of the cilia, in turn, stimulates the rod in a way that generates nerve signals. The signals, finally, are transmitted to the brain stem in a fraction of a second, by the nerve fibers of the rods.

These fibers merge to form the cochlear nerve, which ends in the brain stem.

Inside each side of the brain stem there are two clusters, or nuclei, of nerve cells that receive signals sent by the cochlear nerve. One cluster transmits a fresh set of nerve signals *directly* up to the auditory (hearing) area of the temporal lobe of the brain (H in Figure 6).

The other brain-stem cluster sends signals *indirectly* to the cortex via one of the basal ganglia called the thalamus (Chapter 3). The thalamus and cortex, working together, make sense out of the nerve signals. This is how we immediately understand the meaning of spoken words, recognize common sounds, and appreciate music.

Two deep parts of the brain play a role in memories and emotional responses evoked by sounds, particularly by music. They are the amygdala, part of the brain's emotional circuits (discussed in Chapter XIII), and the hippocampus, which is part of our memory circuit (see Chapter 14). They, I suspect, are responsible for making people cry when listening to extraordinarily moving music or music that has past significance to them.

Composers of great music even wrote in certain keys to inspire specific emotions. I remember this from listening to Boris Goldovsky's comments on various operas, during Texaco's Saturday radio broadcasts, a few years ago. As I recall, G major evokes happiness; G minor, certain kinds of distress; and F minor, gloom.

Common sense tells us that the brain is not "wired" in exactly the same way in all people when it comes to sensing sounds. This is why some people are born with a true sense of pitch and the ability to compose and play music far better than others, and why others are tone deaf even though they can hear perfectly well.

The ear has a large influence on our sense of *balance* as well as hearing. Close to the snail shell there are three small curved tubes, or canals, of bone that open into the fluid-filled vestibule. Each hollow tube forms a loop that is set at a different angle from the other loops, and each one is filled with the same ear fluid that fills the vestibule (Figure 20).

When you change the position of your head, the pressure of the fluid in each loop is altered slightly. There are special cells inside the loops that are concerned with balance and detect these changes. They react by sending nerve signals along the *vestibular nerve* to the brain stem. Nerve cells in the brain stem then relay these signals to the other parts of the brain concerned with balance, including the cerebellum, at the back of the head, which is one of the most important links in the brain's circuits for balance.

What disturbances of hearing and balance does the clinician see?

What are some of the common symptoms, and how is the source of trouble diagnosed?

Deafness, the most common symptom of ear trouble, may be caused by wax in the ear; hardening of the joints between its three movable bones, *otosclerosis;* nerve disease, *neuritis* in the cochlea nerve; or an injury, infection, or tumor in or very close to the ear. A tumor inside the head, *acoustic neurinoma,* that presses on the eighth cranial nerve is another cause of deafness, as explained in my book on these tumors. Constant ringing in an ear, *tinnitus* is another common symptom and may be caused by any of the troubles just listed.

Severe dizziness, *vertigo,* is cause by disturbances of the fluid-filled balance loops—as in seasickness—or by diseases and tumors that alter the function of the vestibular (balance) nerve. Mild dizziness, "Light-headedness," may be caused by various disturbances that upset the brain such as pressure from a blood clot or tumor, low blood sugar, low blood pressure, and certain kinds of epileptic spells.

How is the nature and location of trouble diagnosed? The first order of business is to inspect the ear with an *otoscope.* Is the ear plugged with wax? Is the eardrum inflamed or perforated? The next step is to get an idea of how deaf the ear is and what part of it is out of order.

A crude measure of deafness depends on how well each ear hears a whispered sound as compared to the other ear. A vibrating tuning fork helps localize the source of trouble. If its sound is heard when it is pressed against the bone behind the ear, the hearing nerve is working. If the same person cannot hear the vibrating fork when it is held in the air close to his ear, his deafness must be caused by trouble between the eardrum and the cochlea, which detects sound vibrations. The most likely source of this trouble is otosclerosis.

There is a battery of highly sophisticated tests that can pinpoint the location and nature of trouble with greater accuracy. They rely on calibrated audiometers, which send sounds to an ear in accurately measured decibels. The degree of any hearing loss can thus be scientifically determined rather than guessed.

A more recent test depends on electrical recordings from the brain stem when calibrated sounds are directed at first one ear and then the other. The technique of recording is similar to that used in a standard electroencephalogram (EEG), except that the recording electrodes are placed over the back of the head close to the ears.

Testing the vestibular nerves begins with careful observation of the patient's general behavior. Does he sway to one side when standing with both feet close together and his eyes shut? Do his eyes jerk rapidly from side to side when looking far to the right or left? Other tests that reveal trouble with the balance circuits, and the nature and location of the trouble, include irrigation and rotation tests.

If you irrigate the ear of a normal person with warm and then cool water, he will lean to one side with the warm water and to the other side with the cool. The change of temperature warms or cools the ear fluid that flows through the balance loops of the ear, thus causing them to upset the normal sense of balance. If the irrigation test fails to make a person lean over, this indicates that something is wrong with the balance system.

Rotation tests can temporarily upset the sense of balance and result in jerky movements of the eyes. If they fail to do so, this is another sign of trouble in the balance circuits. The simplest rotation test is to have the patient turn rapidly around and around in circles a few times. This upsets the normal circulation of ear fluid in the balance loops of the ears, and thus makes a person feel dizzy, briefly, and have difficulty in walking a straight line. Children know what this feels like after rolling over and over down a long hill. Another rotation test is to whirl the person around a few times in a special chair. Not a pleasant test, as I know from having tried it.

I, like others, have often wondered how ballet dancers and Olympic figure skaters, after whirling round and round in some of their numbers, manage to keep their balance and not fall over, as many of us would. The explanation, which is a guess, involves the same reasons that some people never get seasick: They get so accustomed to unusual motion that they don't let it bother them, and they are probably endowed with a balance system that is far less sensitive to the effects of rapid rotation than that of many other people. They also learn to focus on just one object each time they complete a turn and thus pay little attention to the rest of the environment.

Additional diagnostic tests include X rays and one of the scan tests (Figure 30) described in Chapter 16.

Once the nature and location of hearing or balance trouble has been determined, efforts to cure it are, of course, the next step. This may call for vitamin therapy to restore function to an eighth cranial nerve, antibiotics to combat an infection, surgery to correct otosclerosis or to remove a tumor, or the use of a hearing aid, depending on the nature of the trouble. An exciting new treatment for some kinds of deafness is to insert fine microelectrodes permanently inside the coils of the cochlea. A sound detector outside the ear picks up sounds and translates them into electrical signals. These signals are transmitted by wires to the microelectrodes in the cochlea. Its receptor organs convert the electrical signals into nerve signals for hearing. While this technique does not restore perfect hearing, it has been of significant help.

The ear, then, is not just for hearing. It is also necessary for your sense of balance. No one knows why these two senses are combined in the ear. My guess, from an evolutionary point of view, is that the close relationship between hearing and balance was important for survival. On hearing the sound of an approaching predator, for example, it was essential for an animal to have a perfect sense of balance for its muscles to function immediately in a well coordinated manner, so that it could flee from danger as fast as possible.

It is the province of knowledge to speak.

—OLIVER WENDELL HOLMES

CHAPTER 12

You Said It

No one knows how or why humans learned to speak. Dr. Lewis Thomas, physician and author, suggests that the constant babble of children may have led to a gradual evolution of sound symbols that became words. Others think that perhaps grunts and other sounds uttered by cavemen became associated with given acts and objects and thus became words. Regardless of speculations about the origin of language, we know that speech is a unique function of the human brain and is made possible by specific areas of the brain.

It is common knowledge that in right-handed people the most important areas for speech are in the left side of their brain. Conversely, in left-handed people the important speech areas are in the right side of the brain. In some people there is no obvious dominance and both sides are involved. As a result, such people often suffer from some form of speech disability or dyslexia. Reversing the letters of a word is a common difficulty. "Dog" becomes "god," and vice versa.

71

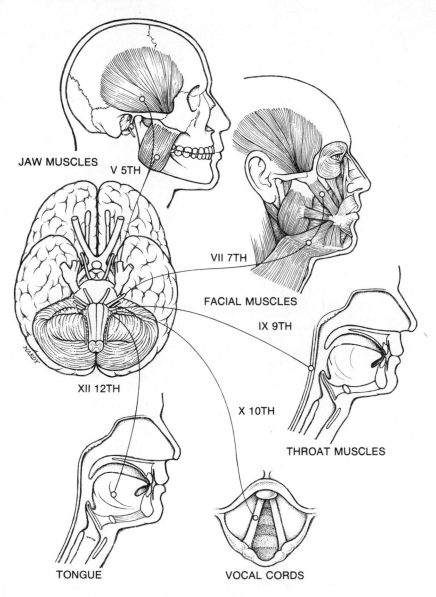

JAW MUSCLES

V 5TH

VII 7TH

FACIAL MUSCLES

IX 9TH

XII 12TH

X 10TH

THROAT MUSCLES

TONGUE

VOCAL CORDS

Figure 22. The ten cranial nerves for speech.

Phonation, the mechanical or physical aspect of talking, involves a surprisingly large number of nerves. We use ten cranial nerves in pronouncing words so that they can be distinctly heard. These ten nerves, five on each side of the brain stem, are the fifth, seventh, ninth, tenth, and twelfth cranial nerves (Table 1 and Figure 22). If you want to see how they work, try saying, "Big cat" in a strong clear voice, as slowly and carefully as you can. Start with your mouth closed.

To open your mouth so that you can make your words clearly audible, the right and left fifth cranial nerves are involved. They control the jaw muscles that close the mouth and also allow it to open.

The first two letters of the word *big* require a *B* sound. To make it, you will find that you have to close your lips and then quickly open them to literally pop out the sound. The lip muscles are controlled by the facial, or seventh cranial, nerves.

The *G* sound in *big* depends on the throat, or pharynx, muscles. If you gently press on each side of your windpipe above the Adam's apple with a thumb and index finger, you can feel these muscles working while you make the *G* sound. They are adjusted by the ninth cranial nerves.

The sound for the *C* in *cat* also depends on some of the pharynx muscles and, like most sounds, on adjustments of the vocal cords as well. The vocal cords resemble the reeds of a wind instrument and are located inside the *voice box*, or *larynx*, under the Adam's apple. They are moved closer together or farther apart by muscles that are worked by branches of the two tenth cranial nerves, the *vagus* ("wandering") nerves. They earned this name because they have many branches, some of which "wander" all the way to the heart and stomach.

The only way you can possibly make the *T* sound in *cat* is to start with the tip of your tongue touching the roof of your mouth. Try saying *T* without doing this; you can't. The tongue is moved by the right and left twelfth cranial nerves.

Speech, of course, depends on air being forced up the windpipe past the vocal cords. Our lungs are the bellows that do this. The big muscle under them, called the *diaphragm*, causes them to fill with air and then force the air out as we breathe. Two spinal nerves, the right and left *phrenic nerves*, control the movement of the diaphragm.

Other muscles also help us breathe. They are the muscles of the twenty-four ribs, twelve on each side, which are controlled by the twenty-four rib nerves. This means that altogether it takes thirty-six nerves to enable us to say, loudly and clearly, the two words *big cat*. (If we add the nerves of the belly muscles, which tighten when we force air out of the lungs, there are at least forty nerves that make phonation possible.)

What parts of the brain make all this happen? Nerve-cell clusters in the brain stem, which give rise to the cranial nerves just listed, are, of course, vital parts of the circuits for speech. They, in turn, are closely interconnected with one another so that they coordinate their nerve signals. They are also linked to other brain stem structures such as the olives, which share with the cerebellum the role of making words ring out clearly so that they are not slurred.

The instructions for talking are sent down to the brain stem from cortical areas that assemble nerve signals for speaking, as explained in Chapter 6. A review of these, and related cortical areas, seems appropriate at this point.

The command post for talking is the speech area of the brain, which has several subdivisions. Its rear portion, *Wernicke's area* (W in Figure 6), coordinates incoming signals from the vision and the auditory areas in ways that interpret the meaning of words that are, respectively, seen and heard. If the visual sector of Wernicke's area fails to function, a person who can see perfectly well cannot understand the meaning of even the simplest word he sees; he will, however, have no problem understanding the words he *hears.* I once operated on a patient who had this problem, due to a small blood clot the size of a fifty-cent piece pressing on that part of his brain. After the clot was removed, the man was able to read and understand words normally again.

Likewise, if the auditory section of Wernicke's area is damaged, or the hearing area next to it, the person will not be able to understand the meaning of words he hears.

Electrical stimulation by neurosurgeon George B. Ojeman of another small area (I in Figure 6) has shown that it, too, plays a role in interpreting written as well as spoken words. It has been similarly shown that a bit of the cortex at M stores short-term memory for words—that is, memory for words *just* presented to you in written or spoken form. Final processing of words takes place at P immediately in front of the motor zone, which controls face and lip action. Area P assembles nerve signals that make it possible for us to talk. But we cannot talk until the processing area P stirs *Broca's area* (B, just below) into action. If Broca's area is damaged, a person will not be able to utter a coherent word. This condition is known as *motor aphasia.*

As explained in Chapter 6, combinations of signals from the speech area, and other parts of the brain, are transmitted down to brain-stem stations connected to the nerves that make speech possible. These other parts of the brain, as already mentioned, include the cerebellum and some of the basal ganglia, which see to it that muscles for talking perform in a smooth, orderly manner. Circuits concerned with emotions and memory, described in Chapters 13 and 14, may also be involved, influencing *how* we speak and what we *feel* about words.

With respect to the relationship between emotions, memory, and words, I hark back to the two simple words *big cat.* I like the words for the emotional pleasure they give me, for they conjure up several pleasant feelings almost simultaneously. They stem from an image of a happy fat cat purring on the hearth, an image of the Cheshire cat grinning out of a Tenniel sketch from *Alice in Wonderland,* and memories of a playful pride of lions I watched at close hand in Kenya. Both emotion and memory circuits in my brain are clearly responsible for these associations I have.

Another aspect of memory and its relationship to words is its role in building up our vocabulary—our ability to recognize, understand, and, above all, remember words. In fact, the breadth of an individual's vocabulary has been found to be a measure of his ability to do well in whatever his line of work happens to be. I learned this years ago at the Stevens Institute of Technology, in New Jersey, which had recently made a vocabulary study of fifteen hundred employees of a large corporation and found that the employees who did better in their jobs were those with the larger vocabularies.

One of the great mysteries is how the mind's inner experience is generated by the tissue of the brain. Along with outer space and the atomic nucleus, it is one of the last frontiers of the unknown.

—DR. MYRON A. HOFER,
psychiatrist

CHAPTER 13

Emotions

When do emotions begin? Suppose you were happily dozing in a warm bath when someone suddenly grabbed you by the ankles, held you upside down, and began slapping your bottom. Would you not howl with rage? Babies do when treated in this manner by the obstetrician who delivers them.

It seems to me, therefore, that the first human emotional reaction is a crude expression of *anger,* and that it occurs on Day One. It is thought, however, that babies are not capable at first of true emotional *feelings.* They simply *react* to what is going on inside or around them. They cry or howl from the distress of discomfort, pain, hunger, or being left alone or isolated. They smile, coo, or doze when comfortable and contented.

The first true emotion of a baby, according to Jerome Kagan, a leading authority on children's behavior, is fear, experienced at the age of six to seven months. The capability for other true or "elaborate" emotions—as well as expressions of love, joy, and pleasure—develops during the next ten to twelve months or so, hand in hand with the growth and maturation of the brain. This theory is based on our knowledge of how the brain grows.

After birth the brain grows larger mainly by the growth and twiglike sprouting of the nerve fibers (axons and dendrites) that form its circuits, including circuits that make emotions possible. Consider fear. Kagan points out that the brains of ducklings and puppies grow more rapidly than the brains of human babies. He suggests that this is why ducklings and puppies display evidence of fear at a much earlier age than babies do—ducklings when only three days old and puppies when five weeks old. In other words, it seems that the development of the sense of fear goes hand in hand with the development of the brain. Other, more elaborate emotions—such as love and pleasure—become possible later, as the brain continues to grow and mature.

Evolution is another factor that apparently plays a role in the development of emotions, according to Paul MacLean, M.D., an authority on the evolution of the brain. His studies take us back to the dinosaurs, the first creatures to walk the earth. Their so-called brain was really nothing more than a small collection of interconnected nerve cells that enabled them to survive. Was the tiny dinosaur brain capable of emotions of any sort? If so, this might be a clue as to how, millions of years later, animal and then human emotions developed.

MacLean thinks that dinosaurs probably *were* capable of simple primitive emotional reactions and that the *oldest* part of our brain, in terms of evolution, is modeled on the dinosaur brain. His reasoning, as I understand it, is as follows:

Fossils show that dinosaurs, which were reptiles, had small brains that resemble the brains of reptiles today. Lizards, Dr. MacLean points out, exhibit simple primitive emotional reactions, such as anger and fear. Therefore, he concludes, the brains of dinosaurs, which were, of course, reptilian brains, were probably also capable of these emotional reactions.

Dr. MacLean's extensive studies of lizards' brains show that their anatomy, wiring system, and chemical characteristics so closely resemble those of the hindmost part of the human brain (our brain stem and some of the gray matter close to it) that he has dubbed this oldest part of our brain the *reptilian brain.*

Millions of years ago, long before our ancestors, the cave men, appeared on earth, no creature had a brain that was any larger than this simple reptilian brain. It was good enough for survival—but little else.

Like our brain stem, it kept the heart beating and the lungs breathing, and enabled animals to experience anger and fear so that they could fight or flee from enemies; to sniff, taste, and forage for food; and to indulge in mating, to perpetuate the species. This simple reptilian brain, in a word, was the creature's "survival kit" and nothing more, just as our brain stem is essentially our survival kit.

The next major step in the evolution of the brain, long before it had developed the surface gray matter we call the cortex, was the growth of brain tissue over and around the reptilian brain. Dr. Mac-Lean calls this addition the *limbic brain* because, like a limb, it surrounds and embraces the oldest and much smaller, reptilian part of the brain.

The limbic brain includes the *deep* gray and white matter that is the core of the fully developed brain of animals and humans (Figure 23). It therefore includes the deep clusters of nerve cells that form the basal ganglia and the hypothalamus, mentioned in Chapter 3. This addition to the brain, Dr. MacLean believes, permitted animals, and eventually man, to experience and display true emotions rather than simple primitive emotional *reactions.*

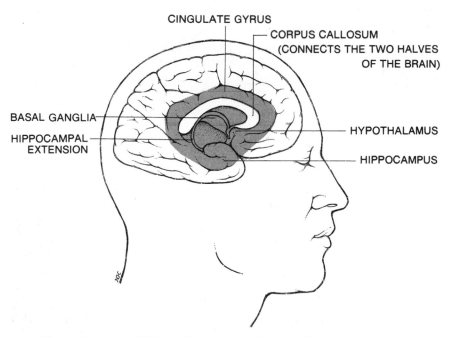

Figure 23. The "Old," or Limbic, brain (gray shading).

The limbic brain also, he thinks, led to more elaborate mating displays and other kinds of body language than those permitted by the simple reptilian brain. It served, too, to coordinate muscular actions and other functions with greater efficiency than the reptilian brain, and it added the hypothalamus, with its thermostat. (Cold-blooded reptiles obviously did not need a thermostat.)

The limbic brain also developed bits of cortex around it. They include the hippocampus deep inside each temporal lobe and the cingulate, or girdling, gyrus over and around the corpus callosum (Figure 23). A major function of the hippocampus is its role in memories concerned with emotions. Each cingulate gyrus, on the other hand, as I have found from observations during operations on or close to them, plays a prominent role in regulating the autonomic nervous system which adjusts the blood pressure, heart rate, breathing, the size of the pupils, and other bodily, or *psychosomatic,* responses that accompany emotional feelings and reactions. These responses are mediated by connections with the hypothalamus, basal ganglia, and brain stem, which are all part of the complex circuits making up the autonomic nervous system.

The cingulate gyri are also responsible for primitive feelings and expressions of such emotions as despair. MacLean, for example, has shown that these gyri are responsible for the isolation cry of an infant animal deserted by its parents. He proved this in two ways: by electrical stimulation of a cingulate gyrus, which evoked an isolation cry; and by removal of the cingulate gyri in infant animals, which prevented them from uttering an isolation cry.

The *neocortex* (*neo* means "new") eventually became the largest and most prominent part of the brain, the command post for the cingulate gyri and other deep, "old" parts of the brain. This made it possible for man and beast to *control* their emotions (although, as we all know, they cannot always do so).

Parts of the limbic brain itself are also responsible for specific emotions. Research studies, for example, have shown that mild electrical stimulation of one of its nerve-cell clusters—the amygdala—causes rats to display ferocious, violent reactions resembling intense anger in humans. On the other hand, if that same part of the limbic brain is removed from each side of the brain of a snarling, vicious wild lynx, as Carl Sagan pointed out, the animal becomes as tame as a pet pussycat.

Stimulation of another cluster, one that is associated with pleasure, causes a cat to purr peacefully and contentedly hour after hour. I have stimulated this so-called pleasure center in a patient suffering intense pain from cancer and had the patient exclaim, "Oh, I feel so good—so good. My pain has gone!"

Scars or tumors affecting other deep nerve-cell clusters of the limbic brain in humans sometimes result in bizarre epileptic spells accompanied by rage so violent that the person threatens to kill members of his family. During operations to relieve certain kinds of epilepsy, electrical stimulation of other deep parts of the limbic brain have induced feelings of pleasure (Penfield and Jasper of Montreal). Observations of this sort of behavior in humans are additional evidence that there are specific and separate deep parts of the brain that control certain emotions.

The most recent addition to the brain in its evolution over millions of years is its largest, uppermost—literally, its "upper crust"—portion, the surface gray matter, or cortex. Technically, it is known as the neocortex, because of its relative newness. It comprises 85 percent of the adult brain and makes it possible for us to cope with life rationally by controlling our primitive emotions, instincts, and reflexes, and by allowing us to think, plan, talk, act, and behave efficiently, and to understand the significance of all the various sensations sent to the brain.

Emotions depend on chemical *transmitter substances* as well as on certain nerve cells and their circuits in the brain. Some nerve cells of the brain and of the pituitary gland, for example, manufacture powerful chemical substances called *endorphins,* meaning internally made (*endo*) morphinelike substances.

When tested on animals, one endorphin stopped pain and calmed the animals; another led to a trancelike state; while still another made the animals irritable and sometimes ferociously angry, according to neuroendocrinologist Roger Guillemin. Such studies suggest that emotions in both animals and humans are probably maintained in a normal, healthy state by the endorphins. It also seems possible that spells of serious sadness, depression, worry, or confusion may be caused by a deficiency or overabundance of some of these "emotional" transmitter substances.

Emotions may be accompanied by two kinds of physical manifestations—*body language,* and changes brought about by *automatic reflexes.*

Body language includes the grimacing, posturing, and gesturing typical of intense anger, fear, or pleasure. Portrait painters are well aware of this. Of the famous painter Giotto, for example, the art critic

Roger Fry wrote, "It is impossible to find in his work a case where the gestures of the hands are not explicit indications of a particular emotion."

Everyone is also familiar with the automatic *reflex* manifestations of emotion—the blush of embarrassment, the pallor of fear, the gasp of surprise, the racing of the heart from stress, and the nasty feeling in the pit of the stomach when a state trooper stops you for speeding. Doctors know, too, that emotional stress can cause serious physical ailments, such as high blood pressure, stomach ulcers, and heart attacks, which, like blushing and pallor, are the result of signals sent to the blood vessels, stomach, and heart by nerves of the autonomic system.

And, as psychiatrist Dr. Myron Hofer has recently pointed out, there is increasing evidence that emotional stress of various kinds can lead to ongoing alterations of body functions, such as enduring changes in metabolism, glandular secretions, appetite, sleep, and disruption of the internal biological clock that governs our twenty-four-hour rhythms. Alterations of this kind, in turn, can lead to such emotional disturbances as anxiety and depression. Mood swings and behavior can also be profoundly influenced by hormones of the pituitary and sex glands, as biologists Evelyn Shaw and Joan Darling have pointed out.

To sum up, our emotions involve a number of factors. Reflex circuits in the oldest part of the brain, the reptilian brain, account for primitive expressions of emotion, such as the rage of newborn babies. Nerve cell clusters deep in the limbic brain are mainly responsible for elaborate emotional reactions and feelings that include pleasure and even ecstasy. These clusters include the amygdala, hippocampus, and hypothalamus (Figure 24). As the figure indicates, emotions may be triggered by sensations of various kinds, ranging from scents, scenes, and sounds to bodily sensations. Figure 24 gives a sketchy idea of the complexity of emotional circuits, which include deep parts of the brain, the "old" cortex or cingulate gyrus, and the "new" or neocortex.

Too little or too much of powerful transmitter substances, including endorphins can also affect our emotions. Physical changes, such as blushing and racing of the heart may accompany emotions. The age, cultural background, and thinking processes of individuals, according to Jerome Kagan, are factors that also influence the range and depth of emotions. Finally, the cortex, the brain's newest portion, is responsible for mastery of the emotions. In this respect the cortex of the frontal lobes is the most important.

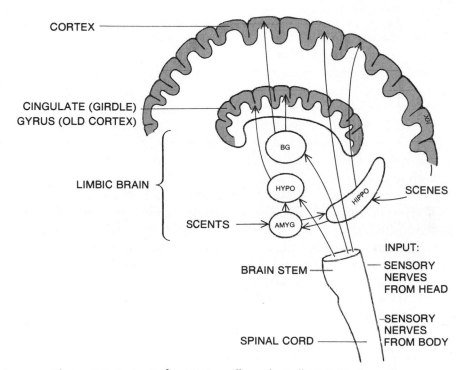

Figure 24. A circuit for emotions (hypothetical). BG: Basal ganglia. Hypo: Hypothalamus. Amyg: Amygdala. Hippo: Hippocampus.

The frontal lobe cortex, however, is also largely responsible for making us *worry* and, perhaps, keep worrying. Prolonged, excessive worry, in some people, can lead to serious and even suicidal depression, or to such extreme and constant neurotic behavior that normal life and feelings become impossible.

Severely crippling emotional and mental illnesses of these and other kinds can be relieved by cutting some of the connections between the frontal cortex and the limbic brain. Such operations, called lobotomies, were once used to permanently relieve such symptoms as chronic anxiety and depression.

The idea of doing lobotomies was suggested by observations of people whose frontal lobes had been badly damaged as a result of an injury or brain tumor. Such people were usually "slaphappy" and free from worry. The aim of a lobotomy, now rarely used, was to reduce worry but not, of course, to cut so many connections that a person was made "slaphappy." When properly performed, lobotomies relieve symptoms without intellectually harming the patient. I know this from having, in the 1950's, performed many.

As to the causes of emotional illnesses, there are many theories. Distressing experiences in childhood may be one cause. Another psychological cause may be more recent emotional shock and distress, as from the death of a beloved member of the family, the piling up of debts, or a drastic business failure. Disturbances of the chemistry of the brain may be another cause, such as the over- or underproduction of endorphins. Withering of nerve cells, especially in parts of the limbic brain—as in Alzheimer's disease—is another cause of some emotional and mental illnesses. Finally, due to genetic decree, the brain of some sufferers of emotional illnesses may be "wired" in a way that makes normal thinking and normal emotional reactions impossible.

In spite of a great deal of ongoing research, there are many more mysteries than answers concerning the causes and treatment of emotional illnesses. There are also more mysteries than answers when it comes to understanding memory, the topic of the next chapter.

Memory, the warder of the brain . . .
    —MACBETH, I, VII, 65

CHAPTER 14

Memory

There are various kinds of memory and various theories as to how they are recorded and stored.

The most primitive kind is *genetic,* or *hereditary memory*—for instance, the grasping and suckling reflexes of newborn infants. Another example of inherited memory is the covering-up reflex of dogs after defecation. Even on a bare, clean city sidewalk they go through the motions, scratching at invisible dirt with their hind legs.

Conditioned reflexes depend on memory. The "Pavlov" dog remembers that food awaits him when the dinner bell rings, and remembers this so well that he drools at the mouth at the mere sound of the bell. And it is my guess that babies develop self-conditioned memories. Once they realize or vaguely remember that crying brings Mama and food to the cribside, they resort to this self-conditioned memory simply as a ploy for attention. As children grow older, other, more elaborate kinds of conditioned memories become important. Avoidance of the stove on which a child has once burned a finger is an example. Toilet training is another.

Jerome Kagan believes that true, or what he calls "active" memory is slow to develop. Memory of a very simple kind, he finds, like repeatedly recognizing an orange ball, is possible when babies are only a few weeks old. But "active" memory, such as remembering where a toy has been hidden, is first evident at about the age of eight months. Children's memory, Kagan believes, like their emotional capacity, matures in step with the maturation of the brain.

What is meant by "maturation of the brain"? As stated earlier, by the time a baby is born, the brain has virtually all the nerve cells it will ever have. Yet it grows larger and more and more capable of learning, remembering, and coping with life situations.

This postnatal increase in the *size* of the brain is mainly due to the growth and branching of more and more dendrites, the trillions of fine whiskery nerve fibers that link nerve cells to one another, according to neuroanatomist Herman Epstein.

The gradual improvement in the *efficiency* of the brain is the result of larger and more effective circuits formed by the newly grown dendrites, and of their slitlike synapses, which transmit their nerve signals.

Recent studies of songbirds, such as canaries and marsh wrens, have proved that dendrites and their synapses actually do grow as the brain matures. Songbirds depend on two small clusters of nerve cells on each side of the brain (those on the left side being the most important) for singing, which is their way of communicating information about their sex, stamina, marital status, territory, and sexual inclinations.

One of these left-sided clusters enables the bird to hear and thus imitate and learn the songs of other birds of its species. The other left-sided cluster enables the bird to sing its own repertoire of songs.

As canaries and marsh wrens grow older, these two nuclei grow larger because of the growth and branching of more dendrites and their synaptic endings, plus the addition of some new neurons. These two nuclei are also larger in birds with a large repertoire of songs than in birds with a small repertoire, and who have 70 percent more synapses, meaning better circuitry, than birds who do not sing at all. In other words, functional and structural maturation of a songbird's brain go hand in hand according to neurophysiologist Fernando Nottebohm. It is believed that the same principle applies to the human brain.

A good deal has been learned about memory in adults from two kinds of observations: observations on what happens when certain parts of the brain are electrically stimulated, and observations on what happens when certain parts have been injured or surgically removed.

Electrical stimulation of the brain is an essential part of certain operations. As explained in Chapter 2, it is used to identify the exact location and limits of a motor area, and can be used on a patient both when asleep and when awake.

Electrical stimulation to outline the speech area, and to locate areas responsible for epileptic seizures so that surgery can be performed, has a bearing on memory processes. This type of test is performed during operations while patients are awake so that they can describe their reactions to the stimulation.

The operations are not painful, because local anesthesia, like that used by dentists to numb a tooth, desensitizes the scalp. Once the scalp is painlessly incised, there is no need for additional anesthesia, because the skull and the brain are not sensitive to pain when touched or operated upon. The patients are, of course, given medicines that have a soothing, calming effect.

Mild electrical stimulation of the speech area is often necessary to outline its exact limits so that it will not be injured during removal of a nearby tumor or scar. Operations of this sort performed by Dr. George A. Ojeman at the University of Washington have shown that *memory for words* is a function of a small word-storage area in the rear portion of the speech area (M in Figure 6).

Memory for past and recent events seems to be a function of the temporal lobes. Electrical stimulation of parts of a temporal lobe, for example, has elicited memories and scenes of patients' pasts, suggesting that this part of the brain is concerned with *long-term memory* (Neurosurgeons Penfield and Erickson).

Removal of a small part of brain tissue close to such an area, from both sides of the brain, however, does not impair long-term memory but permanently makes *short-term* or immediate memory impossible. Such a person, in other words, is forever unable to remember what he had for breakfast on a given morning but can still recall childhood scenes and events. (All long-term memories were obviously once short-term memories. But all short-term memories do not necessarily become long-term. Your short-term memory, which enables you to remember what you had for breakfast today, is not likely to become a long-term memory that allows you, a year from now, to remember that breakfast.)

Observations by Heimer and others suggest that the hippocampus plays an important role in memory by *comparing* memories of the past with recently acquired memories. This does not necessarily mean that the hippocampus is a storage depot for memories. It may simply be an important crossroads between memory circuits.

The cortex directly behind each vision area is responsible for *memories of faces.* After this section of cortex has been damaged, a person no longer recognizes the faces of old friends and cannot remember the faces of new friends.

Complex memories, such as memories of stories, poems, and various past experiences, are apparently largely handled by the forward portions of the brain—its frontal lobes—for these kinds of memory are impaired or lost after serious damage to those parts of the brain.

While certain parts of the brain clearly play a role in some specific types of memory, Neuroanatomist Karl Lashley and others believe that memory in general depends on *many* parts of the brain's cortex *and* its deeper structures working harmoniously together.

Is *everything* we see and experience indelibly recorded in the brain? Probably not, although Dr. Morton Prince, one of America's pioneer psychologists, suggested this possibility. He based this theory on experiments which showed that after being hypnotized, people remembered many more of the objects they'd seen in a room than they had been able to recall before hypnosis. This suggested that *possibly* everything they had seen in the room had been recorded in their brains.

There is no doubt but that everything we see and experience is *signaled* to the brain. This does not mean, however, that everything is permanently recorded there. Common sense indicates that we do not remember thousands of things we see. We can stand on a beach for hours watching ocean waves rolling toward us, but our brain certainly does not indelibly record the pattern of every individual wave. If it did, our memory circuits would surely be so swamped that they would cease to function. In other words, the brain simply forgets trivial, unimportant matters.

Experiments with snails support this theory. Neurobiologist Eric Kandel, for example, has shown that snails continue to react to, and therefore remember, stimuli that are threatening and hence meaningful to them; but they soon stop reacting to stimuli that fail to threaten them. He concludes, therefore, that snails, like people, "unremember" matters that are not important.

What "burns" a memory into the mind? Three factors are obviously important—the vividness of an event, motivation, and attention. Burning one's fingers on a hot stove is a *vivid* event that will long be remembered. And anyone anxious to be a tennis champion clearly has to be highly *motivated* and pay strict *attention* in order to remember and apply all the instructions he receives from a coach.

Howard Gardner, in *The Mind's New Science,* calls attention to other factors that influence memory storage. They include *meanings* and *expectations.* Does a bit of information mean enough to make it worth remembering? Does a person remember it because he thinks or expects it will sometime be useful to him?

There are several theories concerning how memories are recorded. Regardless of which is correct, it seems clear that it takes *time* for a memory to become permanently fixed in the brain. People who have suffered severe brain damage as the result of automobile accidents illustrate this theory. They never remember the cause of the accident, and, depending on how seriously the brain was damaged, they fail to remember events and scenes for hours, even days, preceding the accident. If the brain had not been damaged, it would have had time to fix these memories. Their brain had obviously *registered* scenes and events prior to the accident. These scenes and events would have been permanently recorded as memories if the brain had had the time to function normally.

As to how memories are "fixed," one outmoded theory held that nerve cells underwent chemical changes which fixed a memory much as chemical changes fix images on photographic film.

Three other theories are more plausible. One theory is that memories are coded and stored by *electrical circuits* in the brain, somewhat but not exactly the way memories are stored in a computer. This theory may explain why recent or short-term memories, before they have had time to become long-term memories are wiped out as the result of a severe jolt that causes concussion. The jolt may disturb their electrical circuits, just as dropping a radio out the window disturbs its circuits.

A second theory, advanced by neuropsychologist Mortimer Mishkin and his colleagues, is based on observations of memory studies on animals and humans in whom different parts of the brain have been

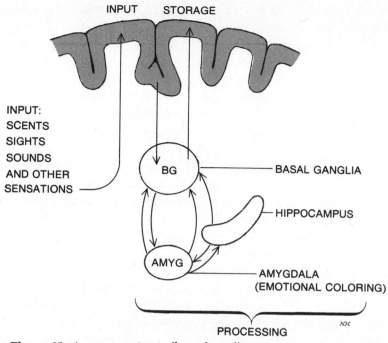

INPUT   STORAGE

INPUT:
SCENTS
SIGHTS
SOUNDS
AND OTHER
SENSATIONS

BG —— BASAL GANGLIA

—— HIPPOCAMPUS

AMYG

—— AMYGDALA
(EMOTIONAL COLORING)

PROCESSING

Figure 25. A memory circuit (hypothetical).

damaged or removed. They believe that memories of *sensations,* such as scents, sounds, scenes, and textures, are stored in the cortex close to the receiving area for each kind of sensation, after being processed by circuits deep in the brain. (Figure 25 shows my interpretation of their theory).

The third theory holds that synapses account for memory fixation and storage. This theory is largely based on studies of rat brains. The brains of rats that have been left alone in a cage and not stimulated into activity have been found to have far fewer synapses than the brains of rats that have lived with other rats, have been extremely active, and have been trained to perform such tasks as threading mazes. This theory is backed by experiments in which slices of a rat's hippocampus have been electrically stimulated by neurophysiologist M. Baudry. New synapses form that greatly increase the number of communications between nerve fibers. In other words, brain activity—whether natural or artificially induced—results in an increased number of synapses, and also, it is believed, in greater efficiency and speed of the transmission of nerve signals by synapses.

Simply stated, the more the brain is used, the better it performs. Think of learning how to swing a golf club or play the piano. Constant practice and repetition presumably cause new synapses to sprout that make the circuits for these activities larger and increasingly effective.

This principle has been applied to the education of children in programs such as Headstart and other early childhood enrichment programs. Headstart children, brought up in an active, stimulating environment, have made and maintained significant gains not only in school but also in college and the job market. Children who have been deprived of a stimulating early environment fall behind all along the way. The 1984 Ypsilante study confirms these findings. It would seem, therefore, that the development of more and more synaptic connections between nerve cells, and between their thousands of interlocking nerve fibers, may well be a major way—if not the major way—in which memory symbols and patterns are coded and stored. This may also explain how learning and memory are related.

Computer experts are trying to use the findings of neurologists to develop ever more sophisticated artificial memories. Daniel Sabbah, senior manager of artificial intelligence at I.B.M.'s Yorktown, N.Y., Research Laboratory, is quoted as saying, "We don't even know how to represent a cat in the computer's memory. We can enter an iconic representation, but the computer would still need the power to generalize—there are cats of different colors and sizes, tigers and house cats, even cartoon cats. . . . Now, specialists are trying to interconnect symbols stored in [computer] memory the way neurons connect ideas in the brain. Silicon circuits, they note, can operate up to a million times faster than neurons. But the brain easily outdistances the electronic circuitry because it can perform thousands of operations at once. Most computers, in contrast, plod along one operation at a time, creating huge information bottlenecks." In fact, Mr. Sabbah continues, "the brain may be the best parallel processor we've got."

We have seen that there are many different kinds of memory, ranging from built-in inherited memories (instincts) to acquired memories such as those of conversations, scents, sounds, literature, and the learning or memorizing of physical skills (e.g., playing the piano or tennis) and intellectual skills (e.g., playing chess or devising computers).

And each type of memory, whether for language, music, vision, taste, or smell apparently has its own brain circuit to encode, process, and store these memories. These individual circuits, of course, interact.

As Proust wrote in the epigraph for Chapter 8, the memory of a taste may evoke memories of scents and scenes. Likewise, circuits for vision and hearing may interact. Eudora Welty, for example, wrote that "Ever since I was first read to, then started reading to myself, there has never been a line read that I didn't *hear.*" Samuel Butler apparently had a keen sense of both visual and hearing (musical) memories that interacted, based on his life-long love of Italy and Handel. In the introduction to Butler's *Selected Essays,* his biographer writes, "Italy and Handel were always present at the bottom of his mind as a kind of double pedal to every thought, word, and deed."

If the day ever comes when these circuits are thoroughly understood, we will know how the mind works. We will know why many older people suffer from very poor memory for recent events but recall childhood events clearly; why some people in their eighties can learn to read music and play the piano; and why a few have what is known as total recall—meaning the ability to remember, for example, exactly what the lady in the red dress said to the lady in the blue dress at a dinner party twelve years ago. Such an ability strongly suggests that the "hard wiring"—the wiring of the brain with which one is born—varies from one person to another.

When memory goes haywire, the result can be utter disaster, as suggested by the title of neurologist Oliver Sacks' fascinating book, *The Man Who Mistook His Wife for a Hat.*

Another aspect of memory, finally, is how memories are recalled. How often have you forgotten a person's name and said to a friend, "I'll think of so-and-so's name in a moment. It will 'come' to me." Moments, minutes, or perhaps hours later the name is suddenly remembered. Does the brain have some sort of cursor that rummages through its subconscious files until—presto!—it comes up with a long-forgotten name? The matter of recall is still another mystery of the "machinery" of memory.

The next chapter considers the intriguing question of whether the right half of the brain, the right brain, has different functions than its left half, the left brain.

After previous investigation of a problem in all directions . . . happy ideas come unexpectedly without effort, like an inspiration.

— HERMANN VON HELMHOLTZ,
   nineteenth-century German physiologist

CHAPTER 15

Left Brain—
Right Brain

If you watch some television announcers *closely,* you can see that movements of the *right* side of their faces are more pronounced than those of the left side. (As noted earlier, the left side of the brain—the *left brain*—controls the right side of the face.) Why is this so? Perhaps because in right-handed people the right facial muscles are stronger than the left, just as their right hand is apt to be stronger than their left.

Another explanation may be related to functions of the left brain. It is thought to be more concerned with practical everyday matters than the right brain, as explained by neurologists Norman Geschwind and Albert Galaburda. So when TV announcers are speaking of such factual matters as news and sports, they are presumably using their left brain more actively than the right. This could account for the greater activity of their right facial muscles.

While the dominant left brain is concerned with practical matters, with speech, and with the critical analysis of facts, figures, events, and ideas, the right brain, is apparently more concerned with *patterns* such as those of paintings, poetry, and musical compositions; with spacial relationships; with emotional *feelings;* and with creative and intuitive *ideas.* It is the artistic, creative, intuitive side of the brain. A cartoon in *Medical Economics,* (14 November, 1983) shows a tycoon and a bored young lady at a café table. Says she, "So much for your financial prowess. Now let's hear something from the *right* side of your brain."

Celebrated examples of intuitive ideas which came while dreaming are Coleridge's poem "Xanadu" and the sudden idea of the carbon-atom ring of the benzene molecule, which is of fundamental importance to modern chemistry, by the German chemist Friedrich Augustus Kekulé (1829-1896). An elegant description of the actual mental processing of a creative idea, quoted by Lord Rothschild, is the following note by Henri Poincaré, French statesman and mathematician, who was trying to solve an extremely difficult mathematical problem at the time:

> For a fortnight I struggled to prove that no functions analagous to those I called Fuchsian could exist. . . .
> Every day I sat down at my work table where I spent an hour or two; I tried a great many combinations and arrived at no result. One evening, contrary to my usual custom, I took black coffee; I could not then go to sleep, ideas swarmed up in clouds; I sensed them clashing until, as it were, a pair would hook together to form a stable combination. By morning I had established the existence of a class of Fuchsian functions—I had only to write up the results, which took a few hours.

Perhaps the ideas of these men materialized during dreams or late at night because the creative right brain was then free to muse without interference from the usually busy practical left brain, which may have been exhausted from a long day's work.

To return to control of each side of the face by the opposite side of the brain, studies of photographs of faces deserve mention. Some fifty years ago there was considerable interest in preparing photographs to portray the face as if it were made up entirely of either its right or left side. This was done by pasting a *mirror image* of the right side of the face over its actual left half. This represented the face as if it were controlled entirely by the left, practical side of the brain. Pictures were made up of two left sides as well.

These composite photographs showed astonishing differences. Right-faced (left brain) photos generally revealed keen, determined expressions and in some instances grim, hard-boiled-looking features. Yet the left-faced (right brain) pictures of the *same* people usually portrayed pleasant, benign, relaxed-looking faces, suggesting an entirely different type of personality.

A recent newspaper item confirms the view that facial expressions often reflect the dominance of one half of the brain. The article reports on the work of psychologist Karl U. Smith of the University of Wisconsin, who studied the faces of hundreds of people using visual observations as well as computerized analyses of lip, tongue, and jaw movements.

" 'My results,' " the article quotes Smith, " 'confirmed that all persons have a sort of facial fingerprint or distinctive way in which they use one side of their face, just as they have distinctive patterns of right- and left-handedness.' "

By this, Professor Smith meant that one side of the face had more prominent furrows around the nose and mouth than the other did, as the result of using the muscles on that side more often and more vigorously. This indicated to him that the side of the brain that controlled the opposite, more active side of the face was itself generally more active than its opposite side.

Nearly 90 percent of all the people he studied were right-faced—meaning they were right-handed, left-brain people. In contrast to this finding, 98 percent of all the opera singers and most of the talented musicians he examined, although right handed, were *left-faced* (that is, right-brain) people.

Moreover, when Smith studied pictures of Beethoven, Brahms, Liszt, and Wagner, as well as videotapes of prominent living musicians, he found that the vast majority of them were also *left-faced*, and hence right-brain people. In other words, most talented musicians are right-brain people while most of the rest of us are apparently left-brain people. It is also thought that talented artists are apt to be right-brain persons, as artist Betty Edwards wrote.

Great achievers, whether in the arts, business, science, or other fields, obviously must rely on *both* their left (practical, driving) brain as well as their right (creative) brain—both sides communicating with each other via the huge number of nerve fibers in the corpus callosum, which links them together.

A vivid illustration that the two halves of the brain can work in harmony as well as independently is seen in Eudora Welty's father, who had the amazing ability to write with both hands at the same time and could simultaneously write the letters either right side up or upside down. In addition, he could write different words with the right hand than those he was writing, at the same time, with his left! This is a clear example of how each half of the brain can function independently of the other. Neuropsychiatrist R. W. Sperry's studies of split-brain people have proved that this is true. When the connections between the two cerebral hemispheres are surgically divided (by cutting the massive corpus callosum and other connecting nerve fibers), neither half of the brain is aware of what the other half is thinking.

It is not surprising that the two halves of the human brain have different functions, for they are not exactly alike anatomically. They differ slightly, for example, in the arrangement of their blood vessels, their patterns of blood flow, and their chemical as well as electrical characteristics.

The two halves of animals' and songbirds' brains have also been shown to have different functions. Most of the nerve cells for recognizing songs, and for singing their own songs, are located in the left brain of canaries and marsh wrens, just as the speech area in right-handed people is located in their left brain. It has also been found that the right brain of rats, like the right brain of humans, is more concerned with spatial relationships and some aspects of emotional behavior than is the left brain.

What's up, doc?

—BUGS BUNNY

CHAPTER 16

Trouble Shooting

So far we have considered the normal brain—what it looks like, what it is made of, and how it works. What about ailments of the brain? How can they be diagnosed and their exact location be determined so that they can be treated and cured? I recently overheard one answer to this question. A man behind me in a bus said to his friend, "My uncle had a blood clot on his brain. How did the doctors know? They threw a CAT scan at him."

No one, of course, can "throw" a CAT scan. The equipment weighs two tons! It is common knowledge, however, that scan tests are widely used to diagnose ailments of the brain as well as the body. To me, who began my training in neurosurgery before scan tests were even dreamed of, they are truly "miracle" tests.

One kind of scan depends on a powerful magnetic field twenty-five thousand times the strength of the earth's magnetic force; another, Positron Emission Tomography (PET), on mildly radioactive emanations from substances absorbed by the brain that are then detected by more than eight thousand miniature sensors around the head. And the CAT scan (or CT scan, as it is now generally called) depends on X rays beamed through the head from six hundred different angles. All these scans, and some other tests I'll describe, rely on computers to analyze the data they receive and to display this information almost instantly as maps or pictures of the brain on paper, film, or TV screen, in either black-and-white or color.

The train of events leading to the use of one or more of these tests usually begins when a person goes to his doctor complaining of severe headaches, double vision, or numbness and weakness of an arm or leg. To get an idea of the patient's trouble, the doctor asks questions concerning the precise nature of symptoms, how long they have been noticed, and whether the patient has had any other symptoms. This is called "taking a history."

The doctor then examines the patient. Do the eyes track normally when looking to right and left? Are the reflexes active, overactive, or as lifeless as those of an English muffin? What parts of the skin are numb? Does inspection of the interior of the eyes supply clues as to the nature of the trouble? If the examination clearly points to brain trouble, the doctor refers the patient to a specialist.

The specialist may be either a neurologist or a neurosurgeon. Both are experts are diagnosing afflictions of any part of the nervous system, be it the brain, spinal cord, or nerves. A neurologist treats patients whose illness requires medicines. A neurosurgeon, obviously, treats those who require surgery. After further questioning and examination of the patient, the neurologist or neurosurgeon arranges one or more special tests to confirm his preliminary diagnosis.

What are these tests? Before describing such new ultramodern tests, let's hark back for a moment to the very first tests, many years ago, that enabled doctors to get an idea of what was going on inside the head without opening it.

The first such test became available about ninety years ago, roughly ten years after the beginnings of modern neurosurgery. It consisted of plain X-ray pictures of the skull that showed its contours as seen from front to back and from side to side. These pictures were made possible by Wilhelm Konrad Roentgen (1843–1923), a German physicist who discovered that X rays cast shadows of bones on photographic film.

While simple X rays do not show the brain or the natural fluid around it, they can show thinning of skull bones that indicates too much pressure in the head as the result of a tumor, blood clot, or some other trouble in the brain. These images occasionally reveal a tumor if it happens to contain flecks of calcium, a substance that does show up on X rays. And when the pineal gland becomes calcified (as mentioned in Chapter 4), X rays will show a shadow in that area of the brain. Displacement of the gland from its usual position is generally a sign of pressure on it by a tumor or clot above, below, or to one side of it. (Simple X rays of the skull, incidentally, are still a routine part of the work-up for patients suspected of harboring brain ailments.)

A big diagnostic leap forward, made early in this century, was the development of *air studies* of the brain. They owe their origin to observations of X rays of skull fractures that had cracked one of the air sinuses around the nose. These pictures showed shadows of air inside the head. The fracture had ripped membranes around the brain and thus allowed brain fluid to leak out of the nose, and air from the nose and one of its sinuses to enter the fluid-filled spaces *around* the brain. The air shadows on these X rays clearly showed the outline of the brain. (Air shows up on X-ray film, as anyone who has looked at X rays of his lungs has seen.)

This observation led doctors to put air deliberately into the spaces around the brain and then take X rays. Air shadows on the film not only outlined the brain but also revealed some afflictions of the brain, such as tumors. Air around the brain is not at all harmful. (Air in blood vessels, however, can be fatal.)

The air was introduced through a needle in the lowest portion of the spinal tunnel, or through a small tube placed in one of the ventricles (1 and 2 in Figure 3). The tube was passed through a small hole drilled in the front or the back of the skull. For both procedures brain fluid was gently exchanged with air, by way of syringe, in repeated small amounts. This was once the only way of delineating the location and character of disorders in the brain without opening the skull. Because it was a painful procedure and often inaccurate, doctors were anxious for better tests.

In the late 1920s two new tests were devised. One was an *arteriogram*, an outline of brain arteries (and veins) on X-ray film. This test, also known as an angiogram, was devised by Professor Egaz Moniz of Lisbon, Portugal, in 1927. A liquid that showed up as shadows on X-rays was injected into one or both carotid arteries in the neck of the patient. (This test, which uses a *contrast* substance, is similar to the use of barium to outline the stomach in X rays.)

An arteriogram depends on a rapid series of X rays taken while the contrast liquid is flowing through the arteries and the veins of the brain. The liquid clearly shows the normal course of the blood vessels; any displacement of them that may indicate pressure from a tumor; obstructions that may cause certain kinds of stroke; and grossly enlarged blood vessels, akin to varicose veins, that sometimes leak blood and result in serious hemorrhage.

Enlargement of a brain artery, because of a congenital weak spot in its wall or because of age or arteriosclerosis, can lead to a bulge (sort of a "blood blister") known as an *aneurysm* (Figures 26a and b). An aneurysm calls for prompt surgery to seal it off. Otherwise, it may burst at any time and result in a fatal massive hemorrhage, as pointed out in my book on brain aneurysms and blood-vessel surgery.

There are other uses of arteriography. It is, for example, essential for guiding microcatheters up inside brain arteries to seal, with a biological "glue," dangerously enlarged blood vessels, which would otherwise have to be removed by surgery.

A recent improvement in arteriography is *digital subtraction angiography* (DSA). *Digital* refers to the digital computer used for this technique. *Subtraction* indicates that the images of all structures, except just one segment of one artery, are erased so that they do not show up

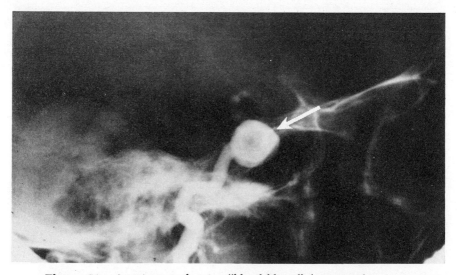

Figure 26a. Arteriogram showing "blood blister" (aneurysm), indicated by large arrow, and its feeding artery (white), indicated by small arrow, in the right side of the head.

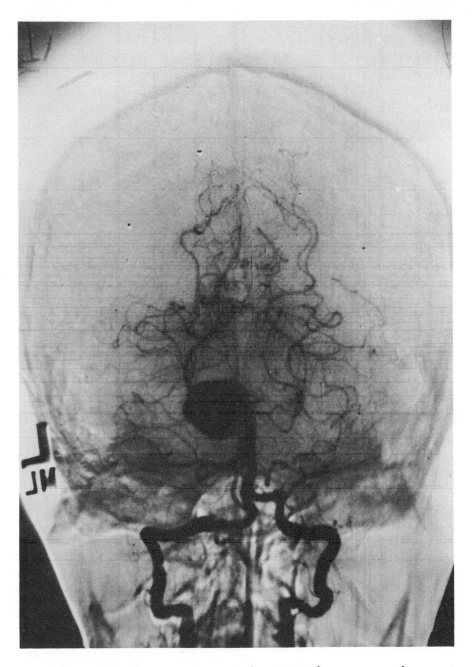

Figure 26b. Subtraction angiogram showing circular aneurysm and blood vessels (black) in the back of the head. *Courtesy of Dr. Edgar M. Housepian.*

on X rays and thus obscure the single artery under scrutiny. The erasure is accomplished by extremely complicated technical maneuvers. DSA is the only way in which some deep arterial disorders can be detected.

Another and very different test for determining the location and nature of brain trouble is the *electroencephalogram,* called an *EEG* for short.

In 1929 the German psychiatrist Hans Berger discovered that the constant ongoing electrical activity of the brain could be amplified and recorded on a roll of moving paper as brain waves, just as the electrical activity of the heart is recorded by an electrocardiogram (EKG). The two procedures are very much alike, both using electrodes applied externally, with no discomfort for the patient, since no injections of air or special liquids are necessary.

An EEG records the electrical activity beneath pairs of recording electrodes placed on the scalp; that is, not the activity of a given nerve cell but the combined output of many cells in a particular region.

The brain's electrical activity is so weak that it must be amplified in order to be recorded by electrically operated pens. The pens are attached by wires to twenty or more electrodes placed over the scalp from front to back and from side to side. A switch box enables the operator of the equipment to direct signals from any two electrodes to a given pen. In this way the operator can record, at will, the electrical activity of different areas of the brain, as shown in Figure 27.

When any part of the cortex is not functioning properly (as a result of injury, disease, or some other cause), the brain waves from that area usually look different from those given off by the rest of the brain. The abnormal waves may be slow and feeble or bursts of unusually large or fast, spiky waves. Abnormal brain waves represent what might be called "static in the attic." Their presence and character can indicate where trouble is located and even what kind of trouble it is. The EEG is especially important in detecting the particular patterns of brain waves that indicate different kinds of epileptic spells, and for monitoring the effects of medicines used to dampen or correct the abnormal electrical activity that causes the spells.

Brain-wave studies, incidentally, show that the brain never sleeps. It is active during sleep even though the pattern of waves is different from that of the brain when one is awake (see Figure 27).

Since the 1950s it has been known that an EEG can pick up and register changes in the electrical pattern of brain waves when a stimulus such as a pinprick or mild electric shock is applied to parts of the body.

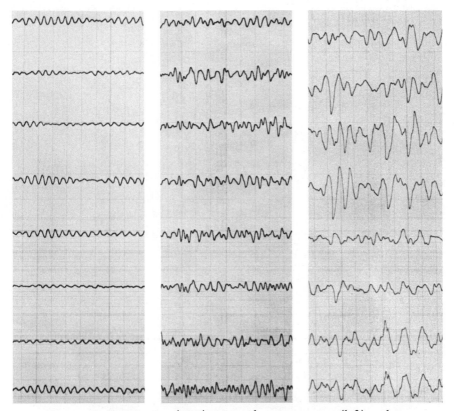

Figure 27. Brain waves (EEG). Normal resting pattern (left), a sleep pattern (center), an epilepsy pattern (right). *Courtesy of Mary Catherine O'Brien.*

This principle has been used for the diagnosis of hearing difficulties, as mentioned in Chapter 10. It is also used, with the aid of a computer, for monitoring surgical procedures close to the brain stem when, for instance, a tumor of the eighth cranial nerve is being removed. If sounds sent into the ear suddenly fail to alter the EEG, this tells the surgeon that he is doing something wrong. He therefore stops operating, waits until sound signals are once more being registered, and then continues the operation in a different way.

This principle has been applied to a kind of monitoring called *Evoked Potential Monitoring* (EPM). When a nerve is electrically stimulated, the stimulation "evokes" an electrical "potential," which travels speedily up to the brain in the form of a spiky electrical wave. Recording electrodes like those used for an EEG can register or monitor these evoked potentials as they reach the brain and, for that matter, as they travel up the spinal cord.

This technique is used during spinal-cord surgery. A leg or foot nerve is rhythmically stimulated and the evoked potentials continually monitored over the spinal cord above the site of the operation or from the brain. If the potentials fail to register, this tells the surgeon that he had better stop doing whatever he is doing and resort to a different, safer approach to removing the tumor.

Another use of the EEG is *computerized,* or *quantitative,* electroencephalography. The computer rapidly averages and analyzes the forms of brain waves, giving a much clearer idea of the various causes and types of epileptic spells than does an ordinary EEG. The computer can also analyze and print out, in color, regions of the brain that are electrically more active than other regions. This is one of the techniques that have shown differences in the electrical activity of the right brain and the left brain.

The use of extremely high-frequency sound waves, *ultrasound,* is another valuable diagnostic aid. These sound waves, when emitted from a compact, hand-held instrument, are detected by an adjacent part of the instrument as they are reflected, in different ways, from different tissues. This is similar to the ways in which aircraft use radar signals and ships use sonar signals. The test enables surgeons during an operation to locate, quickly and accurately, small tumors buried deep in the brain, which would otherwise be difficult to find.

Another of its principal uses is to determine whether a carotid artery in the neck is narrowed or plugged because of arteriosclerosis and is therefore the cause of a stroke. This test is so effective that it has largely replaced the need for arteriography for this purpose. The technique is based on the Doppler principle, which explains why the hoot of a train's whistle changes pitch as the train speeds off into the distance. If there is narrowing or partial plugging in a carotid artery, the flow of blood changes pitch (as reflected in sound waves picked up during the test).

I have had this test and can tell you exactly what it is like. You lie comfortably on a cushioned table. Next to you, in plain sight, is a small TV screen. The technician in charge takes up a small hand-held rod that contains both the sending and the receiving apparatus. He then moves the end of the instrument slowly and carefully over the skin of your neck, over the location of the carotid arteries. Presently, a clear image of the inside of the artery appears, as if by magic, on the TV screen. Any bump or narrowing inside the vessel shows up instantly. I

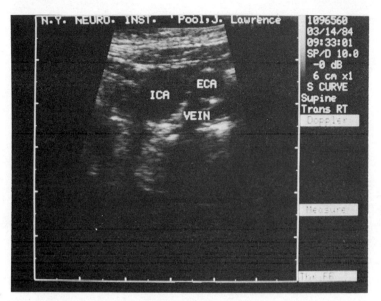

Figure 28. Ultrasound (Doppler) outline of blood vessels in the neck, shown as round black openings. ICA: Internal carotid artery. ECA: External carotid artery. *Courtesy of Dr. J. P. Mohr.*

could see for myself, fortunately, that my neck arteries were wide open and free of any trouble (Figure 28).

Scan tests utilize computers to display information they receive as images on paper, film, or TV screen, in black-and-white or in color. The *CT (or CAT) scan* relies on beams of X rays to reveal outlines of the brain and tissues in and around it. The *PET scan,* explained below, depends on faint emissions from slightly radioactive test substances absorbed by the brain. The *MR (NMI, or NMR,) test,* also described below, requires the use of a powerful magnetic field and radiofrequency waves.

Scan tests owe their invention to efforts in the 1940s to detect brain tumors by "tagging" (labeling) them with mild, temporarily active radioactive substances injected into a vein and then absorbed by a tumor. A Geiger counter held over the scalp registered the concentrations of radioactivity. These crude early efforts to diagnose brain troubles without having to put a needle in the spine for an air study, or into an artery for an arteriogram, were the forerunners of the modern scan tests, which not only are easy on the patient but are highly effective and give instantaneous results. My successor to the chair of neurosur-

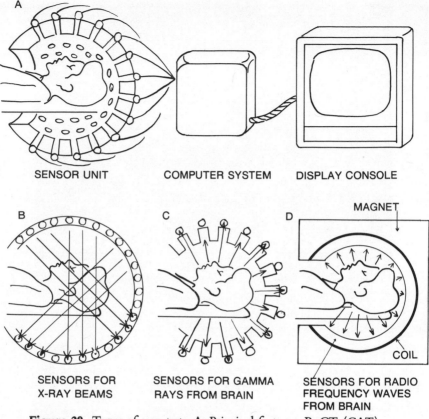

SENSOR UNIT   COMPUTER SYSTEM   DISPLAY CONSOLE

SENSORS FOR   SENSORS FOR GAMMA   SENSORS FOR RADIO
X-RAY BEAMS   RAYS FROM BRAIN   FREQUENCY WAVES
                                          FROM BRAIN

Figure 29. Types of scan tests. A: Principal features. B: CT (CAT) scan. C: PET scan. D: MR (magnetic resonance) scan.

gery at the Columbia-Presbyterian Medical Center, Professor Edward B. Schlesinger, was a prolific contributor to these pioneering efforts.

The CT (CAT) scan. The letters *CT* stand for *computerized tomography*. (The *A* in CAT, standing for *axial,* is no longer widely used). Tomography, from the Greek *tomos,* meaning "slice," indicates that the scan test portrays information in terms of slices of the brain, to show what it looks like as if cut in two—from front to back, top to bottom, or from side to side—at selected intervals.

The test depends on X rays beamed through the brain from six hundred different angles (Figure 29). Sensors on the opposite side of the head detect the beams and relay this information to a computer. The

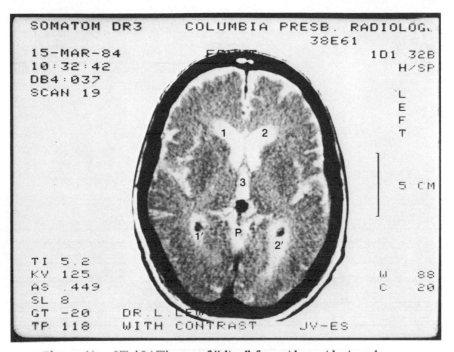

```
SOMATOM DR3        COLUMBIA PRESB. RADIOLOG.
                            38E61
15-MAR-84                               1D1  32B
10:32:42                                H/SP
DB4:037
SCAN 19                                  L
                                         E
                                         F
                                 1   2   T

                                  3        5 CM

                              1'  P
                                      2'

TI  5.2
KV  125
AS  .449
SL  8                                    W    88
GT  -20    DR.L.LEW                      C    20
TP  118    WITH CONTRAST        JV-ES
```

Figure 30a. CT (CAT) scan of "slice," from side to side, just above the uppermost part of each ear. (Photograph of scan). 1 and 2: forward portion of the two largest ventricles of the brain. 1' and 2': hindmost portion of same ventricles. The two small black areas in 1' and 2' are flecks of calcium in the tufts that secrete brain fluid (CSF). 3: Third ventricle (see Fig. 3). P: Calcified pineal gland in normal midline position (see Chapter 4).

Skull bone is outlined in black. Brain fluid (CSF) around brain and in ventricles is white. *Courtesy of Dr. Linda Lewis.*

computer translates this information into outlines of the brain and surrounding tissues. This is made possible because tissues of different densities alter the passage of X rays in different ways characteristic of each kind of tissue, be it bone, or gray matter as in Figure 30a, white matter, or, as in Figure 30b, a brain tumor at the back of the head. The computer displays this information, in turn, on a TV screen or on paper or film. This almost instantaneous method of scanning not only displays or prints out pictures of brain "slices" but also shows brain tumors, blood clots, areas of brain damage caused by a stroke or brain disease, and other abnormalities. The test, incidentally, is not accompanied by any sensations or harmful effects. I know this, having had a CAT scan eighteen years ago just to find out what it was like.

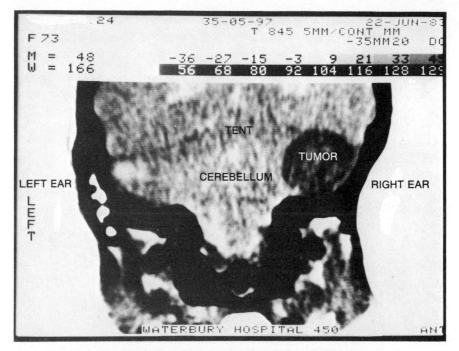

Figure 30b. CT (CAT) scan of back of head, as viewed from front to back. (Photograph of scan). This benign tumor of the right acoustic nerve, inside the skull, was totally removed and patient cured (See Chapter 10). *Courtesy of Dr. James E. Finn.*

CT scans are also used to study other parts of the body, including the spinal cord. The scans are so sensitive that they can portray a cord tumor as small as a lima bean.

Tomography makes sharp "pictures" of one part of the brain at a time by deliberately blurring or erasing the image of neighboring tissues around the slice on which the X-ray beams are being focused. The blurring is accomplished by a complicated method of keeping the beams sharply focused on only one slice of brain at a time.

Three more recently developed scan tests are the PET, SPECT, and MR tests. Each depends on a different principle (Figure 29).

The PET scan. Don't be frightened by the technical name *positron emission tomography* (PET). *Tomography* is defined above, and everyone knows what *emission* means. So let's zero in on *positron*.

A positron is a positively charged electron of an atom. It does not emit anything under ordinary circumstances. But, when the atom is made radioactive, its positrons emit gamma rays. Akin to X rays, but with a shorter wavelength, these rays are detected by devices called *sensors*.

To perform a PET scan, the doctor injects into a patient's vein a very small amount of mildly radioactive substance, such as tagged glucose. (The radioactivity is not strong enough, nor does it last long enough, to be harmful.)

Nerve cells absorb radioactive substances in varying amounts depending on the chemical characteristics of the cell and how active it is. The proportion of gamma rays sent or emitted from tagged cells is detected by sensors around the head.

Nerve cells that become more active than usual send out more gamma rays than do quieter cells. The computer prints out this information in colors that show how active different parts of the brain are at that moment. (Meteorologists use the same trick in their daily weather reports. Radar regions of heavy thunderstorm activity are yellow, heavy rain is red, light rain blue, and areas of balmy weather green.)

The PET test shows that when a person opens his eyes, the vision areas *and* a sizable area of the brain surrounding them "light up." Ask the patient to talk, and his speech area and surrounding brain regions will light up on the scan display. This finding indicates that we should think of such brain functions as vision, speech, and so on, in terms of widespread rather than just precisely localized regions of activity.

The PET scan can also be used to trace the locations and concentrations of transmitter substances (TMs, described in Chapter 6), which are essential for the transmission of nerve signals at the synapses. If deficiency of a certain TM is discovered, it may be a clue to the cause of a serious brain disease.

The SPECT scan. This test, *single photon emission computerized tomography,* is similar to the PET scan except that photons, rather than positrons, are emitted. It reveals how much blood is flowing through various parts of the brain at a given moment, as does another test for this purpose, the cerebrograph.

The cerebrograph. This test monitors regional blood flow (RBF) after the patient has inhaled a small amount of radioactive, but otherwise inert, xenon gas. Thirty-two sensors close to and around the head pick up faint radiations from the circulating blood, thus depicting how strong the blood flow is in the various brain areas. This is one of the scan tests used for detecting early signs of Alzheimer's disease and other disorders in which blood flow may be unusually slow in deep areas of the brain.

The MR (NMR or NMI) scan. MR stands for *magnetic resonance.* (The acronyms NMR and NMI mean, respectively, *nuclear magnetic resonance* and *nuclear magnetic imaging.* The word nuclear, in this instance, refers to the nucleus of the atoms that comprise the brain fluid and the chemical molecules in brain tissues and cells).

The test relies on technical wizardry that alters the spin of electrons in an atom's nucleus in such a way as to make that atom send out radiofrequency signals, much as if the atoms were mini radio-transmitter stations. When these signals are detected by sensors around the head, they are analyzed instantly by a computer and converted into maps of the brain resembling the slices shown by a CT scan. The imaging of an MR scan is, however, in some ways superior to that of a CT scan. It shows brain anatomy, tumors, and other brain disturbances far more clearly. It can also detect and measure regional differences in brain chemistry in ways that other tests cannot. This explains why it, too, is beginning to throw light on the causes and possible cures of mysterious ailments like Alzheimer's disease and distressing motor afflictions caused by trouble in deep parts of the brain.

The MR test depends on two simultaneously active forces, neither of which are in the least harmful to a person—nor does he even feel them. One is a magnetic field, which, as already stated, is twenty-five thousand times more powerful than the earth's magnetic field. In addition to this, radio waves are beamed through the brain. Alone, neither of these two forces have any effect on the brain. But in combination they alter the spin of electrons in hydrogen and other atoms in nerve cells. The disturbed, resonant, or "excited," atoms thereupon send out radiofrequency waves. The source and concentration of these waves are detected by sensors and analyzed by a computer that prints out this information as outlines of deep and surface areas of the brain (Figure 31) and their chemical characteristics. Thanks to Dr. Sadek Hilal, Director of Neuroradiology at the Neurological Institute of New York, the Columbia-Presbyterian Medical Center has the world's most powerful and versatile diagnostic MR unit.

Three different types of equipment can be used to create the

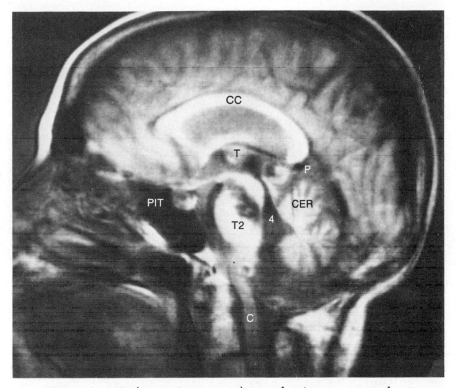

Figure 31. MR (magnetic resonance) scan, showing two extremely rare kinds of deep brain tumor. CC: Corpus callosum. Pit: Pituitary gland. P: Pineal gland. 4: Fourth ventricle. CER: Cerebellum. C: Spinal cord. T: Small tumor in third ventricle. T 2: Second tumor in brain stem. *Courtesy of Dr. Edgar M. Housepian and Dr. Sadek Hilal.*

magnetic field. One is a huge, very heavy permanent magnet, similar in principle to a horseshoe magnet one can buy in a toy store. Another relies on a series of electrically driven resistive coils, like giant doughnuts, with a total weight of three to five tons. The third and most elaborate type depends on the superconducting properties of coils wound with rare metals such as titanium alloys. When cooled to slightly less than absolute zero an electrical current in the coil, and the magnetic field created by this current, continue without requiring any more electricity. Considerable amounts of liquid nitrogen and liquid helium, however, are needed to keep the coils ultracold.

As a result of this and the other tests mentioned, the secrets of brain circuits and brain chemistry are being revealed as if the brain were in a glass box. The multimillion-dollar equipment for doing these tests will, I believe, pay for itself in terms of saving lives and restoring a normal or virtually normal life to thousands of people who are crippled by brain disease.

In a nutshell, those are the tests doctors use to diagnose troubles in the head. The diagnosis of trouble in the spine, such as a slipped disc, is

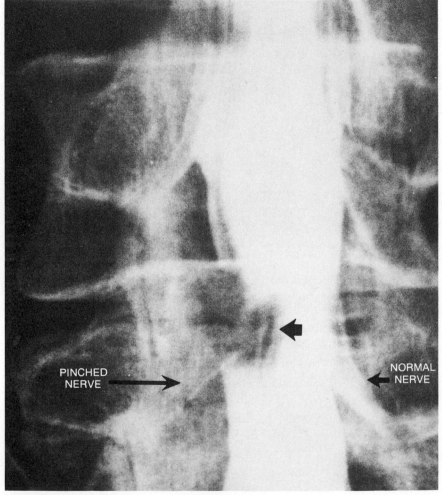

Figure 32. Myelogram with contrast liquid (white) showing "slipped" or herniated disc (arrow). Note that sleeve of the pinched nerve next to the disc is filled by only a thin streak of contrast liquid, whereas opposite normal nerve is clearly outlined. *Courtesy of Drs. H. Gordon Potts and Richard R. Fraser.*

made in much the same way, except that a special test called a *myelo-gram* is commonly used (*myelo* meaning "spinal cord"). A small amount of a liquid, different from that used for an arteriogram, is introduced into the spinal-fluid tunnel at the lower portion of the spine. This liquid shows up on X ray pictures and thus outlines a slipped disc (Figure 32), tumor, or perhaps something else that is the cause of trouble.

This chapter has outlined diagnostic tests. The next step, obviously, is treatment. Ailments of the brain, spinal cord, and nerves that do not require surgery are treated by neurologists, as stated earlier. Those that require surgery are managed by a neurosurgeon. The neurosurgeon's work is the subject of the next chapter.

The most important person in the operating theatre is the patient.

—RUSSELL JOHN HOWARD
English surgeon

CHAPTER 17

Brain and Nerve Surgery

Most operations on the brain are performed to relieve pressure caused either by a growth, by too much brain fluid, or by blood that has leaked from an injured vein or defective artery.

How is brain surgery performed? Let's consider one of the most common kinds of operation—the removal of a benign (noncancerous) tumor, keeping in mind that the patient rather than the surgeon is the most important person in the operating room.

In the doctors' dressing room, the surgeon has just taken off all his ordinary clothes and put on a surgical shirt, pants, cap, mask, and special operating-room (OR) shoes. Stepping into a room next to the OR, he makes sure that all is well with his patient before she is put to sleep. He then scrubs his arms and hands for five minutes before moving into the OR, where a nurse helps him into a sterile gown and surgical gloves.

115

An orderly wheels the patient into the OR. Sterilized sheets are then draped over the patient from head to toe, except for that part of the head that is to be operated on.

"Everybody ready?" the surgeon asks. The nurse in charge of the surgical instruments and the two young assistant surgeons nod. "Let's go then," he says. Nothing further needs to be said. Everyone knows his job.

One assistant places the fingers of each hand on the patient's scalp and presses down firmly so that it won't bleed when the surgeon incises it (Figure 33). After a couple of inches have been cut, the surgeon applies small clamps along each side of the incision, to prevent bleeding. The assistant then moves his fingers to the next section of scalp to be cut, and so on, until an incision shaped like a small horseshoe has been made. The incised portion of scalp is now lifted out of the way, in much the way you would lift the flap of a coat pocket to see what is inside.

Four holes are now bored in the skull with a drill that automatically stops as soon as a hole has been made. In other words, the drill cannot possibly go too far and injure the brain.

With a specially designed small saw, the bone is cut between the holes. This creates a loose piece of bone, which is lifted out of the way to make a window in the skull through which the surgeon can operate.

He cannot see the brain yet because it is covered by a tough blue membrane, the dura (shown in Figure 33). Very carefully, he cuts through three sides of the dura until its cut portion resembles the page of a book ready to be turned. The surgeon "turns the page" by lifting the dura off the brain.

This exposes the brain and, nestled in it, the tumor. It is round and glistening; the size, shape, and color of a ripe plum. From long experience, the surgeon knows at once that it is not cancerous but is the kind of growth that can easily be peeled away and completely removed.

Before he can remove it, however, he has to shut off the arteries that supply it with blood and then the veins that drain blood from it. Before cutting these blood vessels in two, he seals them with the light touch of an electric cautery or with small metal clips resembling miniature clothespins (Figure 33). The tumor is then gently separated from the brain and removed. Some tumors require laser beam surgery.

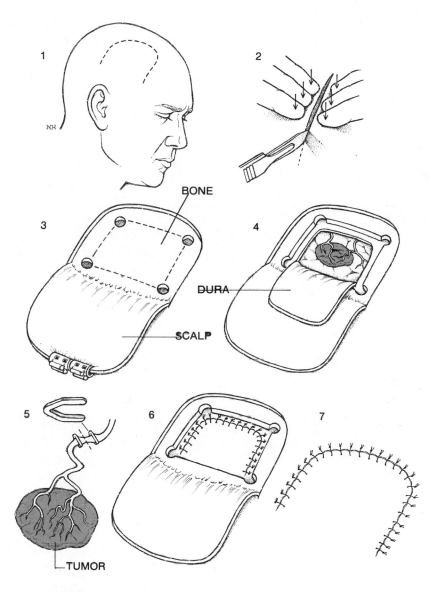

Figure 33. Operation for removal of a brain tumor. 1: Scalp incision.
2: Assistant's fingers pressing on scalp edges to prevent bleeding until
special clips are applied to the scalp for the duration of the operation.
3: Bone ready for removal. 4: Flap of dura opened to expose the brain.
5: Small metal clips are used to shut off blood vessels around the
tumor. 6: Dura stitched after removal of tumor. 7: Scalp stitched after
the removed section of bone has been replaced.

To complete the operation, the surgeon replaces the flap of dura and stitches it in place so that it is watertight and will not allow brain fluid to leak out. The bone and scalp are also replaced in their original positions, and finally the cut edges of the scalp are stitched neatly together. The operation has taken about two hours. When the patient wakes up, the surgeon is happy to find that she is in excellent condition both physically and mentally.

Operations on the brain to remove a blood clot, or a scar that is the cause of epilepsy, or to treat other ailments, are done in much the same way. Operations to remove a slipped disc obviously require spinal surgery.

In my opinion, the greatest advances in brain surgery in recent years have been operations to prevent or remedy causes and symptoms of strokes. Carotid arteries in the neck that have become plugged by arteriosclerosis are one cause of stroke. The arteries can be opened, cleaned out, and sewed up so that, again, they provide a normal supply of blood to the brain.

Small brain arteries that have become plugged are another cause of stroke. A fresh supply of blood to the brain can be provided by connecting an artery outside the skull to an artery of the brain. (I happened to be the first in the world, in 1951, ever to do such a procedure, using a plastic tube, as described in my book on brain aneurysms.)

There are three ways of bringing a fresh supply of blood to the brain: stitching an artery of the temple directly to a brain artery; welding the two arteries together with a laser beam; or using a vein as a conduit between an artery outside the skull and a brain artery. All three methods entail the use of microsurgery, described below.

Another common cause of stroke is bleeding in the head from a defective blood vessel. A massive blood clot from an artery that has burst, because of extremely high blood pressure, can be removed by brain surgery, although often brain damage is severe, and recovery is rare.

There are, however, two blood-vessel conditions that lead to leakage of blood in or around the brain which can be cured by surgery. One of them is the bulging of an artery so that it forms an aneurysm (Figures 26a and b). The other is enlargement of blood vessels, similar, in a way, to varicose veins. If either of them leak blood they cause sudden severe headache, stiffness of the neck, and perhaps other symptoms such as numbness or paralysis of an arm or leg. If they leak blood once they are apt to leak again at any time, often with a massive and fatal hemorrhage. They are therefore literally time bombs within the head that call for prompt surgery to seal or remove them. Methods for treating them are described in my book on aneurysms and vascular malformations of the brain.

For some of these operations, the neurosurgeon peers, while he operates, through a powerful binocular microscope that makes the small twig of a brain artery look as large as a lead pencil, just as powerful bird glasses make a sparrow look as large as an eagle. This kind of surgery, called *microsurgery,* makes tricky operations in vital parts of the brain far simpler and safer than they were twenty-five years ago, when microscopes were not used for brain surgery.

A neurosurgeon also operates on nerves, usually to repair a nerve that has been accidentally cut or badly damaged by a piece of glass or sharp metal. He begins this kind of operation by opening the skin over the path of the injured nerve and drawing aside the muscles around it until he gets a good look at the nerve and its two cut and frayed ends. He then cuts off the frayed ends and stitches the two clean, healthy-looking ends neatly together. Tiny stitches are placed only through the sleeve that covers the nerve, not through the core of the nerve where new nerve fibers grow. It takes a few weeks for new fibers to grow down into the lower, damaged portion of the nerve from its upper healthy portion, so it's usually a few weeks before the patient recovers from the numbness and weakness caused by the accident. Laser beams are now being used, instead of stitches, to "weld" together the two cut ends of an injured nerve.

A somewhat different type of operation is sometimes used to re-store movement to the face after one side of it has been paralyzed by an injury to the facial nerve. A person so afflicted cannot talk clearly or drink properly, because the paralyzed side of the face droops in a limp, unsightly fashion, and he does not have control of that side of his mouth. When the facial nerve cannot be repaired like an arm or leg nerve, one way of restoring power is to connect part of the neighboring tongue nerve to the facial nerve.

To do this, a portion of the tongue nerve is cut across so that its cut end can be stitched to the end of the facial nerve after it has been cut in two.

Nerve fibers from the healthy tongue nerve will now grow down inside the facial nerve to the lip and face muscles that had been para-lyzed. After a few weeks the person can once more move and control his face muscles. But to do so he has to *think* about moving his *tongue,* not his face. After a few more weeks, however, he can *automatically* move his face muscles quite well. (His tongue, incidentally, continues to function because it still has some nerve supply.)

Other kinds of operations that brain surgeons perform include a precise needling of the brain, called *stereotaxic surgery,* for the relief of pain and uncontrollable distressing muscle movements; and the permanent insertion of implanted electrodes for electrical stimulation of parts of the brain. Stereotaxic needling is also used for obtaining samples, called biopsies, from diseased areas or from tumors deep in the brain.

Stereotaxic surgery is a fine art that requires thorough familiarity with the anatomy of deep structures in the brain and exquisite accuracy in the introduction of slender electrodes used to deliberately destroy small, deep areas of the brain that are responsible for pain or muscle disorders. After a small opening has been made in the skull for the passage of the electrodes, a special machine is fixed to the head. Then, after elaborate calculations and X-ray studies, the electrode is gently slipped into the brain at the desired location. The passage of the electrode, or a slender probe carrying it, causes no brain damage, because surrounding tissue is pushed aside rather than torn.

Fine wires for stimulating the brain's vision areas have been permanently put in place in hopes of restoring at least some measure of vision to the blind. Photosensitive detectors outside the head pick up images and translate the images into electrical signals, which are transmitted by wires, led through the scalp to the visual cortex. At this time, this procedure, affords only a crude sense of vision, but it promises, with improvement, to be useful in the future.

Another use of implanted electrodes is their introduction into the coils of the cochlea of a deaf ear. Sounds are translated into electrical signals that activate the special cochlear cells for hearing. This procedure has proved useful in restoring some degree of hearing to some deaf people, and shows considerable promise for improvement in the future.

Finally, permanently placed electrodes, either deep in the brain or over the spinal cord, are being used to alleviate extremely severe pain, just as the electrodes of a pacemaker are used to alleviate irregularities of the heart.

From the brain only, arise our pleasures, joys, laughter, and jests, as well as our sorrow, pain, griefs, and tears. . . . I hold that the brain is the most powerful organ of the human body.

—HIPPOCRATES

CHAPTER 18

Who Discovered the Brain?

Who "discovered" the brain and learned how it works? Many people, over the course of many years. A few of them are listed in this chapter to give you an idea of how people of different historical eras and different nationalities have contributed to the gradual accumulation of our knowledge of the brain.

Cavemen and, later, warriors, who had bashed in the heads of enemies were obviously the first men to have *seen* what the human brain—or at least parts of it—looked like.

Priests, like those of ancient Egypt who dissected sheep to predict the future by studying their organs, and who removed human brains in preparing mummies, obviously must have been familiar with the appearance of brain tissue. Some of them applied this knowledge, scanty as it was, to simple kinds of brain surgery, such as boring a hole in the skull to relieve pressure in the head. We know this because a trephine and other instruments for brain surgery are carved on the wall of an Egyptian temple that is nearly four thousand years old.

Some men of this culture became interested in the brain and nerves, and in how they worked. They were the first lay doctors. Others who wondered about how the brain worked were philosophers. While some of them thought that the brain was the organ of intellect, most thought that emotions were functions of other organs (Cecelia C. Mettler, medical historian).

Democritus (460–362 B.C.), for example, believed that intellect depended on "soul atoms" in the head but that soul atoms of the heart were responsible for such emotions as fear, pride, and courage, while liver atoms were concerned with lust and greed.

Plato (427–347? B.C.), spoke of a "rational soul," meaning the intellect, as being in the head, anger in the heart, and greed in the belly. Others thought that the heart was the source of both intellect and love. These antique ideas have persisted to some extent to the present as indicated by the expression "I love you with all my heart" and the term "gutless" for cowards.

With respect to the anatomy and functions of the brain, Anaxagoras (500–428 B.C.), of Asia Minor and Athens, was one of the first to describe the fluid-filled caves of the brain and to study the brain in an embryo.

Hippocrates (460–377 B.C.), the wise and famous Greek physician of the island of Cos, clearly realized that the brain was the organ of the intellect and consciousness and that its right side controlled the left side of the body, and vice versa. He was also aware that the fluid-filled caves of the brain, when distended, resulted in hydrocephalus. He knew, too, that disturbances of the brain caused epileptic convulsions.

Aristotle (384–322 B.C.), basing his views on dissections of lions and other animals, thought that nerves were sinews or tendons, as his contemporaries also believed.

Herophilus of Alexandria (335–280 B.C.), the "father of brain anatomy," described the largest part of the brain, the cerebrum; its smaller part, the cerebellum; the brain's fluid-filled caves; and the three membranes that cover it. He also described its major veins, including the largest, at the back of the head. Because the blood in it resembled wine in a wine press, it was called the *torcula*, meaning "wine press." It still bears his name today, as the *torcula of Herophilus*. Unlike Aristotle, he knew the difference between nerves and sinews, and even knew that some nerves were for sensation and others for moving muscles.

Soranus of Rome, who lived around 50 A.D., called attention to some, but not all, of the nerves of the brain (the cranial nerves) and correctly stated that the spinal cord was an extension of the brain.

Then came Galen (130–200), the most famous physician of ancient times after Hippocrates and Herophilus. He was born in Pergamon, north of Ephesus on the coast of Asia Minor.

Galen moved to Rome, where he dissected the brains, spinal cords, and nerves of Barbary apes, pigs, and other animals, to learn about their anatomy. He *proved* that nerves control muscles and are not sinews. He also discovered the voice nerves on either side of the larynx, which are branches of the vagus, or tenth cranial nerve. After he severed them, a pig could no longer squeal, nor a dog bark, nor an ape howl. He described seven pairs of cranial nerves (but not the twelve that are actually present) and was the first to call attention to the sympathetic nerves that are part of the autonomic nervous system. The deep innermost large vein of the brain that he described is known to this day as the *great vein of Galen.*

The Middle Ages, which followed the fall of the Roman Empire, was as dormant a period for medicine and anatomy as it was for science and the arts. With the Renaissance, however, there came a fresh burst of interest in investigations of the brain and nerves.

Leonardo da Vinci (1452–1515), for example, dissected and illustrated the nerves of the human body so well that I have used his drawings to illustrate a lecture on the sciatic nerve and its branches. He even found time to experiment on the nerves of animals.

Berengario da Carpi (1470–1530), another Renaissance man, was not only the first modern brain surgeon but an anatomist as well. His dissections of more than one hundred brains led to a clear description of the pituitary and pineal glands, the small fluid-filled cavity in the center of the brain known as the third ventricle, and some of the deep clusters of nerve cells known as the basal ganglia.

Berengario must have been an extraordinarily ingenious fellow, judging from a believe-it-or-not account of how he went about finding whether the victim of a head injury had suffered a fracture of the skull.

Berengario tied a loop in one end of the hair of a horse's tail. He slipped the loop over an upper front tooth of his patient, pulled the hair as tight as a violin string, and then twanged the hair. If the patient had a cracked skull, he would feel pain at the fracture site and point to it.

To explain the pain, I can only guess that the vibrations set up by the taut hair were transmitted from the tooth to the skull bones, just as the vibrations of a tuning fork are readily transmitted by bone. No pain would be caused if there was no fracture. But if there was a crack or cracks in the skull, the bone at that location might be a little loose so that it could be jarred by the vibrations and irritate pain nerves in the dura. Skull bones have no pain nerves, but the dura, which covers the brain, does have a few, in certain locations.

Discovery of the cells of the brain was made possible by the microscope, which was invented by the Dutchman Anton van Leewenhoek (1623–1723). Robert Hooke of England (1635–1703) gazed through a primitive microscope at what he called the "little boxes" in a piece of cork and termed them *cells,* a name that has stuck. Marcello Malpighi (1628–1694), an Italian, through studying fish brains with a microscope, was the first to note that brain tissue contained cells—and also nerve fibers.

Thomas Willis (1622–1675), born shortly after the death of Shakespeare, was the great English physician and anatomist who devoted much of his attention to dissections of the brain and nerves, and to studying the blood supply of the brain. He described the circular arrangement of the important arteries at the base of the brain, which to this day is called the *circle of Willis.* It is a structure of vital importance to neurosurgeons when operating on aneurysms. His dissections of nerves running from the brain to the heart, stomach, and other organs stand out as additional monuments to his work.

Many of the illustrations of the brain in Willis's works were drawn by Christopher Wren (1632–1723) before Wren designed Saint Paul's Cathedral and his other architectural landmarks. The versatile Wren not only prepared anatomical diagrams for Willis but actually shared in some of the dissecting as well.

A milestone in the understanding of the nervous system was the discovery—by the Italian Luigi Galvani (1737–1798)—that muscles contracted when touched by two different metals. His contemporary, Alessandro Volta (1745–1827), pointed out, correctly, that the contractions were the result of an electrical current generated by the two metals and not by the muscles, as Galvani had thought.

The discovery that muscles responded to an electrical current paved the way for electrical stimulation of nerves and the brain, which revealed how they function. Gustav Fritsch (1838–1897) and Eduard Hitzig (1838–1902), both of Germany, were the first to stimulate the animal brain electrically and prove that certain areas controlled muscles of the opposite arm and leg. This was the forerunner of modern techniques that make it possible to learn how individual nerve cells function, tiny as they are, by inserting microelectrodes inside them in order to stimulate them or record their electrical activity.

The Englishman John Hunter (1728–1793) was a famous pioneer in surgery, anatomy, and experimental studies. His ruthless scientific interest is illustrated by his keeping track, year after year, of the whereabouts of a man known as the "Irish Giant" so that he could obtain an autopsy after he died and find out why this huge man was over seven feet tall and so big-boned. The autopsy, performed by Hunter, revealed a large tumor of the pituitary gland. This finding proved to be a milestone in the understanding of the gland and, eventually, of the growth hormone that had caused the excessive growth of bone and stature known as acromegaly.

François Magendie of France (1783–1855) proved that the forward nerve roots of the spinal cord are *motor roots* while the hindmost are *sensory roots.*

The formal study of brain chemistry, which has led to the discovery of transmitter substances and endorphins as well as of so many other chemical aspects of the brain's functions, began about one hundred years ago, thanks to the German physician Johann L. W. Thudichum (1828–1901). He actually did most of his work in London, where he became particularly interested in fatlike chemicals that were found only in the brain. His work so impressed the British government that in 1874 it began to support his studies. This was apparently the first example, now common, of government subsidy for scientific research. (In his later years, Thudichum wrote books on gourmet cooking. They, however, were not subsidized by the government!)

Others who made important early contributions to the chemistry of the nervous system included an English physiologist, Thomas Elliott, who in 1905 described the effects of adrenaline on the sympathetic nervous system; and Otto Loewi, (1873–1945) who in 1921 discovered a substance, released by branches of the vagus, that slowed the heart. He named it *Vagusstoff.* Sir Henry Dale, in 1929, found that this "vagus-stuff" was a complex chemical substance, now called *acetylcholine,* a transmitter substance (TM) not only for nerves of the heart but also for other nerves and for many parts of the brain.

Meanwhile Ramon y Cajal of Madrid (1852–1934) described in exquisite detail all the many *different* kinds of cells of the brain and their connections. Beginning medical school at age sixteen, he devoted his entire life to this study. As a tribute to his national and worldwide fame, Madrid's huge new brain and nerve research center is named the Instituto Ramon y Cajal.

The last one hundred years or so mark a century of rapidly increasing knowledge of how the brain functions, based on observations

of people afflicted with strokes, brain tumors, epilepsy, and other ailments; on electrical stimulation of different parts of the brain; and on
research of the intricate details concerning the anatomy, chemistry, and
physiology of the brain.

Strokes that damaged parts of the brain were carefully studied by
a talented French physician, Paul Broca (1824–1880) a little over a
century ago. His observations were the first to establish firmly that a
specific area was responsible for the ability to utter coherent speech. In
right-handed people it is in the lower rear portion of the *left* frontal
lobe (Figure 6). It is known to this day as *Broca's area*. It is in the
corresponding location of the brain in left-handers.

As more knowledge concerning the function of specific brain areas
accumulated, it soon became possible to figure out where some brain
tumors were located to operate on them. This was in the 1880s, even
before the advent of X rays and other tests like those used today.

Sir Victor Horsley (1857–1916) was the most famous of the
"modern" school of neurosurgeons who *successfully* removed brain and
spinal-cord tumors. With a research colleague, Dr. R. H. Clark, he also
devised a complex apparatus for needling various deep parts of the
brain with pinpoint accuracy. Electrical stimulation or local destruction
of these small areas yielded clues to their functions. Modifications of the
apparatus, which is known as the Horsley–Clark stereotaxic apparatus,
have led to its use in all neurosurgical centers in the world today for
treating crippling muscular disorders, for pain relief, and for taking cell
samples to find out exactly what kind of disease afflicts the brain so
that an effective type of treatment can be instituted.

Neurologists, psychiatrists, neurosurgeons, and research workers
have all added to this growing store of knowledge. It is far beyond the
scope of this book to list them all, although the names and contributions of some of the foremost research workers have been mentioned.

Neurologists have discovered methods of treating distressing and
sometimes fatal muscle disorders such as myasthenia gravis, Parkinson's
disease, and some kinds of epilepsy by medications that were unheard
of twenty or so years ago. And they are working diligently to find the
cause and cure of such baffling ailments as Alzheimer's disease, multiple
sclerosis, and "Lou Gehrig's disease" (amyotrophic lateral sclerosis of
the spinal cord).

Psychiatrists, too, have made spectacular advances in their methods of treating mental and emotional illnesses. Two hundred years ago
"insane" people were simply confined to asylums like London's Bethle-

hem Royal Hospital (popularly known as "Bedlam"). Early in this century, at a hospital in New Jersey, schizophrenic patients were treated, for a while, by having their entire colon removed. It was thought that perhaps toxic substances absorbed from the large bowel were the cause of symptoms! In the 1950s shock treatment, meaning convulsions induced by the injection of insulin or the application of electrodes to the head, became popular. And, at about the same time, lobotomies were frequently used to alleviate the profound anxiety and agitation of some kinds of mental illness. Both these kinds of treatment are still used, but only occasionally, after all other appropriate methods have been tried and failed.

Today treatment of many mental illnesses and serious mood swings is being managed by medications of new and more effective kinds than those of past years. Nor must we forget, in this thumbnail sketch of advances in psychotherapy, the role of psychoanalysis, stemming from Sigmund Freud and his followers, as well as his dissenters.

Neurosurgeons have likewise made significant contributions. Harvey Cushing (1869-1939), one of the world's greatest brain surgeons, showed that there are various types of pituitary-gland tumors and that excessive hormone production of each kind of tumor can lead to different physical symptoms and signs. One tumor can abolish sexual interest and capability; another can cause the breasts of women who are not pregnant nor yet a mother to produce milk; a third can lead to bodily weakness and loss of weight; while a fourth can make a person put on pounds and pounds of fat and develop an extremely high blood pressure.

Wilder Penfield (1891-1976), founder of the Montreal Neurological Institute, was another giant in the field of neurosurgery. He and his colleagues, during countless studies of patients with epilepsy, showed that electrical stimulation of certain parts of the brain, as stated earlier, resulted in emotional and memory responses. These observations added greatly to our knowledge of brain circuits and Professor Paul C. Bucy (1904-), now editor of *Surgical Neurology*, conducted a series of brilliant studies, reported in 1944, that outlined the complex motor circuits of the brain. Others who have made notable discoveries of brain areas and their functions are vividly described by John Green, Professor of Neurosurgery at the Barrows Neurological Institute, Phoenix, Arizona.

Increasingly accurate scan tests of various kinds now make it possible to look at separate regions of the brain almost as if they were enclosed in a glass box. These tests can reveal local changes of the brain's blood flow, chemistry, fluid content, electrical activity, and transmitter substances in such detail that it is possible to make early diagnoses of illnesses such as certain kinds of stroke, Alzheimer's disease, and so on, paving the way to better methods of treatment hitherto undreamed of.

Spectacular discoveries of neurotransmitters and how they work have opened up new and better ways of treating brain ailments for which there was no adequate treatment ten years ago. They include more effective ways of treating emotional and mental illnesses, epilepsy, disturbances of the endocrine glands, and muscle disorders like Parkinson's disease and myasthenia gravis.

Recent studies suggest that new synapses can form in ways that make learning and memory possible. This has led to the theory that the brain is not, as formerly thought, "wired" in an entirely fixed way, but is capable of adjustments by the formation of new circuits. This so-called *plasticity* of brain circuits explains, it is believed, why some people may recover functions that have been lost as the result of a serious head injury or stroke.

As a result of all this newly acquired knowledge, doctors can now cure or improve the lives of thousands of people suffering from all kinds of brain, nerve, and muscle ailments that could not be successfully treated ten years ago.

What of the future? We can only guess. I believe, however, that it is reasonable to think several major advances are likely to take place. Certainly, some will be made through genetic engineering—the study of genes that cause brain and nerve ailments, possibly leading to their correction by replacing the causative genes with other genes. Genetic engineering has already paved the way to the artificial manufacture of growth and other hormones, and should, I think, make considerably more progress in this direction in the future.

Steadily improving diagnostic scan and other tests promise earlier diagnoses, before there has been permanent brain damage, and therefore far more effective treatment of brain, nerve, and muscle diseases in the future. Finally, the field of immunology, as it applies to brain chemistry, promises new and better chemical substances with which to treat mental and emotional symptoms like depression, violent behavior, and perhaps eventually, such presently incurable diseases as Alzheimer's disease and schizophrenia.

The transplantation of young nerve cells into old brains, I believe, is now on the threshold of developments that in time may be spectacular. And improvements in methods of electrically stimulating nerves and parts of the brain to restore lost functions will, I think, be another major advance in the future. After all, permanently implanted electrodes have already been used for this purpose, although they have not yet proved highly satisfactory.

Two things are certain about the future. One is that the study of the nervous system, the study known as neurobiology, will continue to expand and come forth with new helpful ideas and therapeutic developments. The other is that there will remain more mysteries than answers as to how the brain, and hence the mind, works. There will remain, in a word, an element of magic as to how and why the brain is capable of thoughts, feelings, and memories.

Glossary

Adrenal gland The gland over the kidneys that secretes the hormones adrenaline and natural cortisone.

Amygdala The cluster of nerve cells, deep in the brain, concerned with memory, emotions, and the senses of smell and taste.

Angiography X-ray outline of the brain's (and other) arteries.

Autonomic Nervous System (ANS) The "automatic" nervous system, which automatically controls blood pressure, heart rate, breathing, and many other vital bodily functions.

Axon The single well-insulated nerve fiber of a nerve cell which sends its most important nerve signals.

Basal ganglia Clusters of nerve cells, deep in the core of the brain, concerned with motor, sensory, and other functions. Part of the limbic brain.

Brain The cerebrum, cerebellum, and brain stem.

Brain stem The lowermost, hindmost, and oldest part of the brain.

Cerebellum The part of the brain at the back of the head under the tent.

Cerebrospinal fluid (CSF) The fluid that fills the ventricles of the brain, permeates the brain substance, and surrounds the brain and spinal cord.

Cerebrum The largest, uppermost, and newest part of the brain.

Cingulate gyrus The girdling gyrus ("old" cortex) over the corpus callosum.

Circuits The interconnected nerve cells of the brain (and spinal cord), concerned with special functions.

Cochlea The snail shell–shaped bone in the ear that controls hearing.

Convolutions The gyri of the surface of the brain.

Corpus callosum The large bundle of nerve fibers that connects the two halves of the cerebrum.

Cortex The surface gray matter of the cerebrum and cerebellum.

Cranial nerves Nerves of the brain, twelve on each side.

Dendrites The branching nerve fibers of a nerve cell that receive and send nerve signals.

Disc The cushion of cartilage between each bone or vertebra of the spine. When it bulges or "slips" out of place, it is often called a slipped or herniated disc.

Dura The tough blue membrane that lines the skull and the tunnel in the spine, and also forms the two partitions inside the head.

Dyslexia   A reading disability, of which there are several kinds, caused by various kinds of faulty brain function.

Echo test   An ultrasound test for outlining normal and abnormal structures in the head and spine.

Electrodes, implanted   Electrical wires placed or implanted in the brain or other parts of the body.

Electroencephalogram (EEG)   Recording of the electrical activity of the brain.

Electromyogram   Electrical recording of muscle activity.

End organs   Small structures at the ends of nerve fibers, for detecting sensations of various kinds.

Endorphins   Chemical transmitters, for nerve signals, made by cells of the brain and pituitary gland.

Falx   The sickle-shaped partition between the right and left halves of the brain.

Fibers, nerve   see *Nerve fibers*.

Ganglion (plural: ganglia)   A cluster of nerve cells.

Glial cells   The cells that support the brain and also have other functions.

Gray matter   Parts of the brain and spinal cord that look gray because they are composed of densely packed nerve cells.

Gyri   The surface "humps," or convolutions, of the brain.

Hippocampus   The seahorse-shaped structure deep in each temporal lobe of the brain, concerned with memory, emotions, and other functions. Part of the limbic-brain cortex.

Hypothalamus   An important station of nerve cells, located under the thalamus and between the brain stem and the cerebrum, dictating control of life-sustaining functions via the autonomic nervous system.

Lobes of brain   Frontal lobes: the brain's forward portions. Temporal lobes: inside the temples of the head. Parietal lobes: halfway between front and back of the head. Occipital, or hindmost, lobes: at the back of brain, containing the vision areas.

Medulla   The lowermost part of the brain stem.

Melatonin   The hormone of the pineal gland that slows sexual activity.

Meninges   The two transparent membranes that cover the brain and spinal cord.

Microsurgery   Surgery performed while peering through a powerful binocular microscope.

Midbrain   Forward portion of the brain stem.

Myelin   Insulating substance around nerve fibers.

Myelogram   X-ray test that outlines the spinal cord and structures such as a "slipped disc" close to the cord.

Neocortex   The newest part of the cortex in terms of evolution. The rim of gray matter covering the cerebrum.

Nerve cell   A cell that sends and receives nerve signals. A *neuron*.

Nerve fibers   The "wires" of nerve cells, which transmit nerve signals. Axons and dendrites are nerve fibers. Nerves are made up of nerve fibers.

Nerve signal   An electrical and chemical process by which nerve cells and nerves communicate.

Nerves, autonomic   See *Autonomic nervous system.*

Nerves, cranial   See *Cranial nerves.*

Nerves, spinal   See *Spinal nerves.*

Neuron   Nerve cell.

Neurotransmitter   see Transmitter substance (TM).

Pons   The midportion of the brain stem.

Spinal nerves   Nerves of the spinal cord, to and from parts of the body.

Synapse   The gap between ends of dendrites and axons through which nerve signals are transmitted.

Tent   The tent-shaped partition at the back of the head, covering the cerebellum.

Transmitter substance (TM)   Also called *Neurotransmitter.* Chemical substance necessary to transmit nerve signals across synapse gaps.

Ventricles   The four fluid-filled "caves" in the core of the brain.

Vestibule   The fluid-filled cavity inside each inner eardrum.

White matter   The white matter of the brain and spinal cord is composed of nerve fibers (the "wires" of nerve cells) and the glial cells that support and hold together the brain and spinal cord.

References

Chapter 1

Cowan, Maxwell. "The Development of the Brain." In *The Brain*. New York: Scientific American, 1979.

Iversen, Leslie L. "The Chemistry of the Brain." Ibid.

Chapter 2

Nauta, Walle J. H.; and Feirtag, Michael. "The Organization of the Brain." Ibid.

Chapter 3

Bucy, C. Paul. *The Precentral Cortex*. Urbana, Ill.: University of Illinois Press, 1944.

Chapter 4

Ehrenkranz, Joel R. L. "A Gland for All Seasons." *Natural History*, June 1983.

Post, Kalman D.; Jackson, I. M. D.; and Reichlin, S. *The Pituitary Adenoma*. New York and London: Plenum Medical Book Company, 1980.

Waldhauser, Franz; and Wurtman, Richard J. *The Secretion and Actions of Melatonin*. Vol. 10, *Biochemical Actions of Hormones*. New York: Academic Press, 1983.

Chapter 5

Duffy, Philip E. *Astrocytes: Normal, Reactive, and Neoplastic*. New York: Raven Press, 1985.

Nauta and Feirtag. See Chapter 2.

Sagan, Carl. *The Dragons of Eden. Speculations on the Evolution of Human Intelligence*. New York: Random House, Inc., 1977.

Chapter 6

Kandel, Eric R. *Cellular Mechanisms of Neuronal Function*. San Francisco: W. H. Freeman and Co., 1976.

Kandel, Eric R. and Schwartz, James H. *Principles of Neural Science*. New York: Elsevier/North-Holland, 1981.

Snyder, Solomon H. "The Molecular Basis of Communication between Cells." *Scientific American*, October 1985.

Chapter 8

Heimer, Lennart. *The Human Brain and Spinal Cord*. New York and Berlin: Springer-Verlag, 1983.

Chapter 9

Doty, Richard L. *Mammalian Olfaction, Reproductive Processes and Behavior.* New York and London: Academic Press, 1976.

Thomas, Lewis. *Late Night Thoughts on Listening to Mahler's Ninth Symphony.* New York: Viking Press, 1980.

Chapter 10

Barlow, H. B.; and Molton, J. D. *The Senses.* Cambridge: Cambridge University Press, 1984.

Hubel, David H.; and Wiesel, Torsten N. "Brain Mechanisms of Vision." In *The Brain.* New York: Scientific American, 1979.

McDermott, Jeanne. "Researchers Find There Is More to Vision Than Meets the Eye." *Smithsonian,* April 1985.

Chapter 11

Pool, J. L. *Acoustic Neurinomas. Early Diagnosis and Treatment.* 2d ed. Springfield Ill: Charles C. Thomas Co., 1970.

Chapter 12

Ojeman, George B. Cortical Representation of Speech. Address at the 73rd Annual Meeting of the Society of Neurological Surgeons, 1983. From author's notes.

Chapter 13

Fry, Roger. *Vision and Design.* 5th printing. Cleveland and New York: The World Publishing Company, 1963.

Guillemin, Roger. "Endorphins, Brain Peptides That Act Like Opiates." *New England Journal of Medicine,* Jan. 1977.

Hofer, Myron A. "Relationships as Regulators: A Psycho-Biologic Perspective on Bereavement." *Psychosomatic Medicine,* May/June 1984.

Kagan, Jerome. *The Nature of the Child.* New York: Basic Books, Inc., 1984.

MacLean, Paul D. "The Co-Evolution of the Brain and Family." *Anthroquest* 24, 1982.

Penfield, W. and Jasper, H. Epilepsy and the Functional Anatomy of the Human Brain. Boston, Little, Brown and Co.

Pool, J. L. "The Visceral Brain of Man." *Journal of Neurosurgery* 11(1954): 45–64.

Sagan, Carl. See Chapter 5.

Shaw, Evelean; and Darling, Joan. *Female Strategies.* New York: Walker and Company, 1985.

Chapter 14

Baudry, M., et al. Increase in glutamate receptors following repetitive electrical stimulation of hippocampal slices. *Life Science* 27 (1980): 325–330.

Butler, Samuel. *Selected Essays*. Bedford Square, London: The Travellers' Library, 1927.

Epstein, Herman. "Multimodality, Crossmodality, and Dyslexia." *Annals of Dyslexia*. Vol. 35, 1986.

Gardner, Howard. *The Mind's New Science*, New York: Basic Books, Inc., 1985.

Heimer, Lennart. See Chapter 8.

Kagan, Jerome. See Chapter 13.

Kandel, Eric R. See Chapter 6.

Lashley, Karl S. "In Search of Engrams." *Society of Experimental Biology* 4, 1950.

Mishkin, M.; Malamut, B.; and Bachevalier, J. *Memories and Habits: Two Neural Systems*. Bethesda, MD: National Institute of Mental Health, 1985.

Nottebohm, Fernando. "Learning, Forgetting, and Brain Repair." In Geschwind and Galaburda. See Chapter 15.

Ojeman, George B. See Chapter 12.

Penfield, Wilder; and Erickson, T. C. *Epilepsy and Cerebral Localization*. Springfield, Ill.: C. C. Thomas, 1941.

Prince, Morton. From author's notebook.

Sanger, David E. "Smart Machines Get Smarter." *The New York Times*, Dec. 15, 1985.

Weikart, David P. et. al. *Changed Lives: The Effects of the Preschool Program on Youths Through Age 19*, Ypsilanti, Michigan: High/Scope Educational Research Foundation, 1984.

Welty, Eudora. *One Writer's Beginnings*. Cambridge: Harvard University Press, 1984.

Chapter 15

Denenberg, Victor H. "Behavioral Asymmetry." In Geschwind and Galaburda, below.

Edwards, Betty. *Drawing on the Right Side of the Brain*. Los Angeles: J. P. Tarcher, Inc., 1979. Distributed by Houghton Mifflin Co., Boston, Mass.

Geschwind, Norman; and Galaburda, Albert M. *Cerebral Dominance. The Biological Foundations*. Cambridge: Harvard University Press, 1984.

Lord Rothschild. *Random Variables*. London: Collins, 1984.

Nottebohm, Fernando. See Chapter 14.

Sacks, Oliver. *The Man Who Mistook His Wife for a Hat*. New York: Summit Books. A Division of Simon & Schuster, Inc., 1985.

Sagan, Carl. See Chapter 5.

Smith, Karl U. Quoted in: "Beethoven, It Seems, Was Very Left-Faced." *The New York Times*, Nov. 27, 1984.

Sperry, R. W. "Lateral Specialization of Cerebral Function in the Surgically Separated Hemispheres." In *The Pyschology of Thinking*. New York: Academic Press, 1973.

Welty, Eudora. See Chapter 14.

Chapter 16

Fitzsimmons, Jeffrey R.; and Mick, Rodney C. "Image Quality and Magnetic Field Strength in NMR Imaging." *Applied Radiology*, April–May, 1985.

Pool, J. L.; and Potts, H. Gordon. *Aneurysms and Arteriovenous Malformations of the Brain. Diagnosis and Treatment.* New York: Harper and Row, 1965.

Chapter 17

Pool, J. L. See Chapter 16.

Chapter 18

Bucy, Paul C. See Chapter 3.

Green, John R. "The Beginnings of Cerebral Localization and Neurological Surgery." *Barrow Neurological Institute* 1, no. 1, 1985. "Cerebral Localization During the Last Century." Ibid, no. 2, 1985.

Fulton, John F. *Harvey Cushing. A Biography.* Springfield, Illinois: C. C. Thomas, 1946.

Mettler, Cecilia C. *The History of Medicine.* Philadelphia and Toronto: The Blakiston Company, 1947.

Penfield, Wilder. See Chapter 14.

Index

About the Author

J. Lawrence Pool, Emeritus Professor of Neurological Surgery, Columbia University, was the Professor and Chairman of that department at the Neurological Institute of New York of the Columbia-Presbyterian Medical Center, from 1949 to 1972.

A graduate of Harvard College in 1928, he obtained his M.D. degree at Columbia's College of Physicians and Surgeons (P & S) in 1932 and then spent seven years training to be a neurosurgeon. In 1941, he was awarded the degree of Doctor of Medical Science by Columbia for research work on the brain.

During WW II Dr. Pool served as the neurosurgeon, for three years (1942–45), with a mobile army field hospital in North Africa, Italy, France, and Germany.

Special professional interests included operations for the removal of acoustic nerve tumors and the surgical treatment of abnormal, life-threatening blood vessels of the brain. Former avocational interests: skiing, fox hunting, seaplane piloting, and ocean racing. In the 1930s, he twice held the U.S. national squash racquets title. Current interests: writing, fly fishing, painting, and golf.

Married, with three sons, he now lives in West Cornwall, Connecticut. In 1985 he became the second American to be awarded a Medal of Honour by the World Federation of Neurological Surgeons.